WITHOUT
THEIR
PERMISSION

WITHOUT THEIR PERMISSION

How the 21st Century Will Be Made, Not Managed

Alexis Ohanian

BUSINESS PLUS

NEW YORK   BOSTON

Business Plus
Hachette Book Group
237 Park Avenue
New York, NY 10017

www.HachetteBookGroup.com

Printed in the United States of America

RRD-C

First Edition: October 2013
10 9 8 7 6 5 4 3 2 1

Business Plus is an imprint of Grand Central Publishing.
The Business Plus name and logo are trademarks of Hachette Book Group, Inc.

Library of Congress Control Number: 2013939396
ISBN 978-1-4555-2002-2

Dedicated to my mother and father,
Anke and Chris Ohanian:
I wish you were here to read this, Mom.
May this book, my life, and my persistent smile
all honor you.

Contents

PART III

A Quick Introductory Note

Hello, I'm a breadpig.

Every company I've helped start has a cute mascot I drew. It's sort of my thing. For this book, the breadpig (a pig with slices of bread for wings) will be the cute spokesmodel to my Bob Barker. It's the eponymous mascot for my social enterprise, Breadpig, which we'll get to in chapter 7 (no peeking!). You'll notice he's black and white, which makes this book a guide for navigating the Internet age successfully *as well as* a coloring book! What a deal!

The World Isn't Flat; the World Wide Web Is

In an August 20, 2011, op-ed piece for *The Wall Street Journal*, world-renowned venture capitalist and tech entrepreneur Marc Andreessen declared that "software is eating the world."[1] I couldn't have said it better myself. Andreessen sets the stage: "With lower startup costs and a vastly expanded market for online services, the result is a global economy that for the first time will be fully digitally wired—the dream of every cyber-visionary of the early 1990s, finally delivered, a full generation later." Software developers worldwide are transforming every single industry on the planet thanks to the open Internet, which makes unprecedented "permissionless innovation"[2] possible even for a couple of twenty-one-year-olds like me and my reddit.com co-founder, Steve Huffman.

My story starts out rather ordinarily. Despite having been born in Brooklyn, I was raised in the "textbook"

---

1. http://online.wsj.com/article/SB10001424053111903480904576512250915629460.html

2. http://www.avc.com/a_vc/2010/02/permissionless-innovation-and-patents.html

suburbs of Columbia, Maryland,[3] and did well enough at my public high school to get into the University of Virginia. It was on move-in day, when I met my roommate, Steve, that things started to get interesting.

By the time we graduated, Steve and I had taken twelve thousand dollars in seed funding from a then unheard-of investment firm called Y Combinator to start reddit.com. Less than a year later, I was organizing meetings with potential acquirers and, in less time than it took me to write my honors thesis, we sold our company to Condé Nast. Sixteen months after graduating from college, I was a millionaire.

Since then, I've founded a social enterprise, helped launch a travel search engine, started a nonprofit corporation, invested in more than sixty startups, advised hundreds more, spoken about tech entrepreneurship all over the world, and helped in the fight against two terrible legislative bills—the Stop Online Piracy Act (SOPA) and the PROTECT IP Act (PIPA), which threatened to undermine the free and open Internet that made my success (and the success of many others, some of whom you'll read about here) possible.

But this isn't just my story. I've had a lot of advantages and a lot of help along the way,[4] but the beauty of the Internet is that you don't need these advantages to change the world. The near ubiquity of the Internet (in the developed

---

3. Seriously. I've met architecture students who've told me that Columbia, Maryland, appears in their textbooks as a model planned community.

4. I describe being a straight white middle-class male born in the USA as "life with cheat codes." Even being tall is an advantage in business, apparently. http://money .cnn.com/2009/07/17/news/companies/tall_book_arianne_cohen_interview .fortune/index.htm

world, for now) has brought with it the promise of a global stage on which ideas can come to fruition. For centuries, invention was limited to those who had access to the means of production and access to labor. Today, you can simply create and present your ideas online. Granted, if it's that easy for you, it's that easy for everyone. Having your content discovered, let alone appreciated, is not guaranteed. There continues to be innovation that will help new and interesting content come to the surface, but even as a work in progress, it's better than the old world of gatekeepers. If there isn't a platform for something yet, chances are someone will build it—soon. The ruthless, fickle, and particular users of the World Wide Web have created the most competitive marketplace of ideas the world has ever seen; you either make something people want or people move on.

Global connectivity isn't just changing the way we do business; it's changing the way we think of value. More than ever, we as individuals have the opportunity to put our ideas into practice without the implicit or material support of traditional communities, industries, and governments. Now any individual—an undergrad at UVA, a comedian from Austin with cerebral palsy, a farmer in Missouri, or a public school teacher from the Bronx—can transform the way we all live. As value creation shifts from well-connected MBAs to the innovators themselves, so does wealth creation. Whatever you think of the world's youngest billionaires, Mark Zuckerberg and his Facebook crew, they're just the beginning. The *Forbes* list of richest people—or its future equivalent—is going to have far fewer businesspeople and far more creators on it. If this seems obvious to you, great: I'll be your Sacagawea-like guide as we meet scores of pioneers in their fields. If this sounds crazy and maybe even a bit shocking, *even better!*

So here's how it's going to go: I'll spend the first part of this book describing my own experiences as a startup founder. You'll learn how I ended up getting involved in all this, how Steve Huffman and I took a failed application to Y Combinator and turned it into reddit, one of the fifty most popular websites in the world. You'll hear about the early days of a travel search engine that had no business being in business with entrenched incumbents, but we started it anyway because we were so damn frustrated.

Then in the second part of the book I'll break it all down so you can do it, too—everything from taking that great idea you had last night over drinks to closing that first round of funding that'll let you quit your job and turn that cocktail concoction into a real business.

The third part of the book covers just about everything else one could aspire to do online. Whether you want to embrace the Internet for fun, profit, or the good of humankind (or all or any of the above), this book has you covered.

There's a unifying message here: the Internet is already doing awesome things, and it's just in its infancy. No one knows what's coming, but we're certain that the status quo is due for some serious disruption and that it's up to the innovators to push us forward. That's where you come in.

I say this not just as an observer but as an active participant. I'm a serial entrepreneur, investor, and adviser. I grew up online, and now the Internet is how I make my living—it went from being my babysitter to being my boss. It's been good to me, and it's good for everyone else, too (yes, incumbents, even you). That's because the Internet helps people help themselves.

It's no surprise to me that the Internet freedom movement has been so successful here in the United States, given that this core message of entrepreneurship is so baked into the founding of our country. Now the platform is connecting us as never before, enabling and empowering innovation that simply wasn't possible because the markets governed by supply and demand never met the need for it so efficiently. Read this book to find out how to chart your own course or to avoid becoming obsolete. I'll share everything that's worked and a few things that have failed spectacularly. Above all, I hope you'll carry this blueprint, and the optimism inherent in it, with you long after you put this book down. It's vital that we preserve a level playing field, not just to keep my book relevant but also for the sake of human progress, which is more important. Nations are making decisions in the coming years about the Internet that will significantly affect the trajectory we'll take politically, economically, and socially.

I'm writing this book to inspire as much as to inform. The Internet has tremendous potential for anyone who works with it. I want to lionize the efforts of some of the innovators who've benefited from this new medium and inspire others to join them in creating something themselves. Generations X and Y were raised to believe that they could be and do anything they wanted. I never did become a professional football player, but when one takes a more rational approach to life goals, the online opportunities become boundless.

There is still a significant digital divide, even in the United States, and certainly in the developing world, but I intend this book to spotlight what happens when a population has its most basic needs fulfilled and can use the Internet for remarkable things. All these are reasons to bridge this divide, whether in Yerevan or Brooklyn. Through connectivity, there is an opportunity of global proportions unlike anything the world has ever seen.

I don't care what Tom Friedman says.

Spherical   Porcine   Flat

A Perfect Marketplace of Ideas

The Internet is an open system: it works because you don't need to ask anyone's permission to be creative and because every address is equally accessible, whether it's the dot-com of the world's largest multinational corporation, the dot-gov of the world's most powerful country, or YourFirstWebsite .com. As former secretary of state Hillary Rodham Clinton said, "Once you're on the Internet, you don't need to be a tycoon or a rock star to have a huge impact on society."

All links are created equal. They have to be. The reason we fight to preserve this openness is because the innovations of the future—whether in business, activism, the arts, politics, philanthropy, or cat photography—cannot come to fruition with anything less. An open Internet means a platform where *what* you know is more valuable than *whom* you know. The promise of such a platform (and the reason we must protect it) is that it allows awesome ideas to win because people like them, not because some gatekeeper said so.

To quote Fred Wilson, a friend of mine and one of the most successful (and best-liked) tech venture capitalists in the country:

> The Internet is not controlled by anyone or anything. It is a highly distributed global network that has at its core the concepts of free speech and individual liberty. This ethos, which includes but is not limited to hacker culture, is in many ways at odds with big companies, institutions, and governments which seek to control, regulate, and "civilize" the Internet.[5]

It's threatening to incumbents, especially lazy ones with something to lose, but that's all the more reason why the supporters of Internet freedom are so numerous.

I'm motivated by all the awesome people whose ideas we've never benefited from because of where they were born or because of their race, sex, or other characteristics. All the bullshit that holds amazing people back doesn't suddenly disappear online, but the open Internet does technologically level the playing field for everyone. When all links are created

---

5. http://www.avc.com/a_vc/2011/06/investing-in-the-cultural-revolution.html

equal, your ideas can win simply because people like them. The future of innovation will be made, not managed. We cannot (and should not) control it. Our responsibility is to get everyone onto the playing field with the skills they need to succeed. We cannot afford to make the wrong decision and stifle Internet freedom—mostly for the sake of human progress but also because I don't know what else I'd do with myself if I didn't have this platform from which to share and develop my ideas.

For incumbents who read this: you don't have control, but that's okay. In fact, you never did—the Internet just demonstrates it in real time. The Internet is a network without hierarchies. And that's awesome. Here's what that means.

We the People, in Order to Form a More Perfect Network

The Internet is a democratic network where all links are created equal. And when such networks get hierarchies forced upon them, they break. They start looking a lot more like the gatekeepers and bureaucracies that stifle great ideas and people in the physical world. That's why we fight so hard to keep them the way they are—open—so that any idea that's good enough can flourish without having to ask anyone's permission.

This is new territory. Before the social media revolution connected billions, this was only hypothetical. Ideas traveled across the Internet, but there was neither the number of users that there are today nor the applications necessary to speed discovery and sharing. Thanks to the emergence of sites like Facebook, Twitter, Tumblr, Pinterest, and reddit, we're now seeing social media play out every day, affecting every business in every industry. And if it's not apparent right now for your industry, it will be soon.

A few years ago, most would have scoffed at the idea that a couple of Rhode Island School of Design graduates in an apartment with laptops would have more rooms available for rent than the Hilton corporation[6] (not *a* Hilton or even the biggest single Hilton hotel—the entire Hilton Hotels empire). But that's exactly what happened. The guys at Airbnb.com (air bed-and-breakfast; see what they did there?) found a brilliant, simple way to connect people who have space, from spare bedrooms to entire homes, with people looking to rent, like vacationers and business travelers, in an online marketplace. These days, their company is valued in the billions and highly profitable. I had the privilege of watching them pitch their idea at Y Combinator Demo Day, if not the foresight to invest in them when I had the chance. Airbnb is a perfect example of a company that *technologically* could've existed before social media connected the web— websites like CouchSurfing.org and even craigslist had been facilitating this for quite some time—but thrived when it did because social media had created a critical mass of people who were comfortable turning online relationships into real-world business transactions.

Five years ago, I doubt you would've found many international hotel companies who were worried about startups

---

6. http://www.forbes.com/sites/bruceupbin/2011/06/29/airbnb-could-have -more-rooms-than-hilton-by-2012/

disrupting their industry. They owned all those expensive, big, solid buildings, after all! It would take ludicrous amounts of money to build a hotel empire in a few years, but that's exactly what Airbnb did—except they did it with pixels rather than bricks. It turned out that a vast empire of hotel rooms was in our homes the whole time.

Airbnb is just one example of disruption enabled by an open Internet, but there are countless others happening as we speak. No one can predict just how these industries will be disrupted—only that it's a matter of when, not if. That's the nature of innovation. We make things that never existed before. In an industry without the biases and inertia of "how things should be done," you'll have a tremendous advantage over incumbents—some of whom won't adapt fast enough, even when they realize they must. That's the free market, online and in hyperdrive—industries disrupted in less than twelve parsecs.[7]

It's Not as Simple as It Looks

So you're convinced these "interwebs" aren't just a fad. Fabulous!

One hitch—none of this future is guaranteed.

In fact, if history is any indication, someone is going to screw it all up. Invariably, whenever a major leap in the American information industry occurs, it first flourishes with openness and innovation but ultimately is swallowed up or consolidated. Tim Wu, author of *The Master Switch*,

---

7. I know. It's a unit of distance, not time—blame George Lucas.

describes the brewing war over the Internet that echoes past battles long lost over telephone, radio, and film. Basically, his book is a downer, but a very important one, that pairs well with my book and a nice Malbec.

We've got something going for us this time, though, and it's not just my youthful optimism. The information platform we, the people, wield is far, far more powerful than any of its predecessors. The United States (and, to an extent, the world) witnessed it firsthand on January 18, 2012, when the Internet went on strike—thousands of websites went dark as thousands of people went to the streets in protest and millions of Americans did something no expert predicted: they won an unprecedented victory against entrenched powers and tens of millions in lobbying dollars. The people who fought against SOPA and PIPA did it in the name of Internet freedom, and it's fitting we succeeded thanks to the platform we fought to protect.

Over the years, whether I'm speaking to Fortune 500 executives or college students, whether I'm talking about the future of nonprofits or entrepreneurship, I've found myself coming back to the same themes. I can't talk about the power of the Internet enough, so I figured I'd take this message to more people than I can fit in a room using the printed word. Why a book? Not many people have the attention span to read something this long online. That, and because books smell so good. This book begins with my own story, which couldn't have been written without HTML.

PART I

The American Dream Lived Online

*"Yes, I'd like to upgrade my dad's season tickets. Oh,
front row, fifty-yard line, please—the best you have."*
Me, approximately three minutes after we sold reddit

Halloween has always been one of my favorite holidays,
but on October 31, 2006, all the hard work Steve Huffman
and I had put into starting reddit (with lots of help from

our first hire and good friend, Dr. Christopher Slowe) had quite literally paid off. The first thing I did after the money showed up in my checking account was to call the Washington Redskins ticket office and upgrade my dad's tickets to something a bit better than the nosebleed seats we had. I then made a sizable donation to my mom's favorite charity and got back to handling all the inbound press. It was a blur of a day, but once it ended, I was able to take stock of just how far we'd come in only sixteen months.

When Steve and I looked at each other, there were no cheers of joy, just a shared sigh of relief. We'd pulled off something statistically improbable—just barely—and we knew it. And after everything we'd been through…wow. Grateful, we went and shared a pizza at Mike's, the same place where we'd been ordering pies since we moved to Somerville, Massachusetts. There, we caught our breath after an entire day of interviews.

For my parents, it was a day when their only child had become a millionaire before he was twenty-four. But they always just wanted me to be happy. Neither one of them really understood the PC they brought into the house not long after my tenth birthday, but they let me do whatever I wanted to it as long as I didn't break it.

Actually, I almost did break it on several occasions, but then I wound up putting it back together. That computer was my gateway to another world once we got a dial-up Internet connection. I campaigned hard for that 33.6Kbps connection, and when I finally got to hear those now-antiquated sounds of the modem, it seemed like magic to my adolescent brain.

This is actually my cousin BJ's computer, but if you thought I looked happy playing on his, imagine how excited I was to get one of my own.

I built my first website on GeoCities. I think it was /sili convalley/hills/4924. It was my fan page for Quake II. There wasn't much going on there beyond some photos of rocket launchers and railguns with a few tacky animated flaming skulls. I really liked that game. But at the footer was a counter that showed how many people had viewed the website (I'd later learn that most of those "views" came from me reloading the page).

But at the time: what power! I could build something from my suburban bedroom and millions (okay, well, hundreds) of people all over the world could see just how much I loved a video game. That's how I got interested in making websites. There was no turning back.

A company called Sidea[1] was my first nonfamilial employer (I suspect the real reason my dad wanted a kid was that he needed someone to do all his yard work—and for well below minimum wage, I might add). I later worked a lot of random jobs between high school and college: Pizza Hut cook and waiter (some of the best customer-service experience one can get), deli counter attendant (I was terrible at this and hated smelling like cold cuts after work, despite how much my dog liked it), FedEx warehouse grunt (great exercise, though not very mentally stimulating), and parking booth attendant (get paid to read books? Yes, please! Until the robots replace humans, that is).

But the job with Sidea was one of the most pivotal I ever had—even if the company went bankrupt a year after I started (not my fault!), a victim of the dot-com bubble bursting.

My job was simple: I had to man a booth in the middle of a CompUSA store, armed with a headset microphone and a large computer monitor. I was to demo software and hardware every thirty minutes—regardless of whether or not anyone was listening. Want to give a fourteen-year-old experience in public speaking? Tell him he has to demo random computer products to an entire CompUSA full of people ignoring him.

I can't tell you how many demos I gave to no one. But I did every one of them as though my boss were watching. In between demos, I killed time browsing the Internet for the latest in Quake II news. For this job I was paid a ludicrous ten dollars per hour. I think I know why Sidea went bust.

But damn if that wasn't a fabulous way for me to start pub-

---

1. https://plus.google.com/+AlexisOhanian/posts/RUdmybEmYSA

lic speaking. If you've experienced the embarrassment of the public speaker's worst-case scenario (speaking to a roomful of people who are both ignoring you and hating you) before you've finished puberty, things are probably going to be okay.

One day I was approached by a man trying to decide between two different mice. I don't recall the details, but there wasn't a big difference between them, save the color and maybe another minor feature. I pitched him on his two options with a quip about the bonus "feature" of a different color. He laughed and offered me a job. He handed me his card and said he'd like to hire me for sales. I kept that card in my wallet for years until it finally disintegrated. Fortunately, I scanned it before it did.

I didn't have the heart to tell the man I was only four-teen. When I told my parents about the offer, they told me to finish high school first. I never called Steve Harper, general sales manager for Stanley Foods, Inc., but I had a hunch I was on the right track. I was always tall for my age, and weighing 260 pounds at the time also helped age me up, as much as being heavy may've sucked the rest of the time.

Being the tallest guy in the class and having a name that's usually given to girls[2] are enough to make a person stand out in school, but make him one of the most overweight as well and you've got a recipe for something. It easily could've gone the other way—self-loathing and depression—but I cared too much about video games and computers to realize how not cool I was.

2. In fact, I was named after a three-time title-winning boxer, Alexis Argüello.

I overcame my weight by making jokes about it before bullies could. Girls were trickier, though. I nearly failed geometry because of a cute girl named Erin, who told me (well, she told my best friend, but so it goes in eighth grade) that I was too fat to go to the dance with.

Like a lot of my not-popular-but-not-pariah peers, we developed personalities and pursued hobbies that interested us, because "just being cute" wasn't an option.

We tinkered on our computers and spent way too much time playing video games with each other. I started a non-profit called FreeAsABird.org that built free custom websites for small nonprofits that had little or no web presence. I e-mailed all my clients cold, and as far as I know they had no idea I was a teenager. After earning a 4.0 my freshman year, I did as little work as I could but still kept my grades up in high school so I could maximize my time spent gaming and running the competitive gaming teams I managed.

Thank goodness, too. Because that was a long-term investment in myself. Most schoolwork felt awfully irrelevant when compared to work that was actually affecting real people and giving me leadership opportunities (albeit digital ones), nurturing the community management skills that would come in handy later (see chapter 2, on co-founding reddit).

Of course, all that time in front of a monitor began to take its toll, as my metabolism wasn't nearly as fast as my buddies'. Our fast-food binges may've done nothing but fuel LAN parties (that's where lots of people bring their computers over to someone's house to connect directly to a local area network—for gaming). True story: I'd never attended a party that didn't have "LAN" in its name until college.

This pattern of eating wasn't healthy. I got tired of being fat by my junior year of high school and decided to do something about it so I could get in good enough shape to play football before I graduated.

Thanks to regular exercise and the abolition of soda and junk food, I lost fifty-nine pounds. My pediatrician (who was always kind of a jerk) couldn't believe it when he read it on the chart. And to this day I can't believe how differently people treat me. To have been the "pear-shaped fat kid" for all those formative years and then join the ranks of the easy-on-the-eyes crowd is like turning on another life cheat code.

One random night, I bumped into Erin (remember—from eighth grade?) at a movie theater—she literally didn't recognize me. It felt great. I may have danced a jig when I got back to my seat to breathlessly tell my friends what had just happened.

There Are Nerds in College

I applied to only one college, the University of Virginia. At the time I didn't give it much thought, but I can't help wondering how much different life would've been if I hadn't made that seemingly insignificant decision. I had no contingency plan aside from the local community college, much to my parents' dismay. I included along with my application a CD-R with my "digital portfolio" on it. It's rather embarrassing, but I've now uploaded it for your viewing pleasure at http://daskapitalcapital.com/my2001portfolio/. I'll wait while you go look.

If you were drinking a cup of coffee at the time, I imagine you did a spit-take. If not, please don't tell me, as I'd like to preserve the image.

Much to my parents' relief, I got in to UVA. But that's not the important part. The decision that defined my experience there and made reddit possible was checking the box for "old dorms" on the housing questionnaire. I didn't know what this meant at the time; old dorms just sounded cooler than new dorms, which were really suites—I wanted something that looked like the colleges I'd seen in movies.

The day we moved in, I spotted a blond-haired guy playing Gran Turismo on his PlayStation 2 across the hall from my new dorm room. His name was Steve Huffman. I was thrilled because I'd worried that no one played video games in college—that this was something I'd have to leave behind as a relic of my childhood. Steve was much less excited to meet me, because he'd seen my name on the door and thought he was living on a co-ed hall. So I was excited that he played video games; he was bummed that I wasn't a girl. He got over that, and we became best friends. Picking old dorms and ending up across the hall from Steve was one of the best, albeit most random, things that ever happened to me.

You've Got to Be Willing to Disrupt (and Be Disrupted)

My dad has been a travel agent for more than thirty years. I distinctly remember dinner-table conversations around the time the Internet started to disrupt the travel industry. As a high school student with a particular interest in computers and technology, I was especially enthralled with all the buzz around the "dot-com bubble."

Dad, on the other hand, was watching his commissions

from airlines get cut all the way to zero. Travel agents used to make good money from bookings that now were going to OTAs (online travel agencies). Because of this disruptive technology, people were now booking their own flights and hotels, cutting out the middlemen—people like my dad.

Just a few years before, my dad decided to leave his position at a large agency to start his own small travel agency. A first-time entrepreneur, he was now facing a dramatic shift in the way his industry did business—and there was no stopping it. The Internet was changing the fundamental business models for the travel industry.

One night he came home from the office particularly frustrated. He'd just learned from a major airline that they, too, would finally be eliminating travel agent commissions altogether. After years of being gashed by these airlines, my father sent them a fax to articulate just how he felt as his business was being eroded.

"Fuck you."

He doesn't remember if he put a cover sheet on that fax, but I like to think he did.

Unlike people in other industries, he couldn't call his lobbyist on K Street and ask him to get a law passed that would make sure all travel agents get a commission. He had to adapt his business model. And he did. To this day, he continues to operate with a focus on business and first-time travelers (usually boomers taking their first cruise). It's not an enterprise I'll be likely to take over, especially given hipmunk (see chapter 3), but it's one he and his employees will, I hope, continue to run for years to come.

But those dinner-table conversations made an impression on me. The Internet was a powerful tool, and I wanted to be sure I knew how to use it. The free market is ruthless. But it has to be. It's up to us to make the most of it.

We must be opportunistic—when disruptions happen we need to identify the new business models and adapt, as my dad did. Or better, we need to be the ones doing the disrupting.

I knew I wanted to be a disrupter.

Sometimes You Just Have to Stand Up

My commercial law professor at the University of Virginia, Professor Wheeler, one day commented in class on the fact that I always volunteered to be the demo person in front of the class when he needed human props. He said how important it was to show up, to stand up—lauding my effort. I just thought it was fun to be that guy in a class of hungover undergrads. It wasn't that I thought I might get better grades, but I figured I had two legs, so why the hell not get up and use them?

I'd never expected to give a TED talk, let alone at twenty-six years old, but then again I'd never expected to be in Mysore, India, which is where I was in October of 2009 as an attendee of TEDIndia, one of the yearly TED presentations that the organizers host all around the world.

A month or so before the conference I was included on a massive e-mail blast from Chris Anderson, curator of the TED Conference, that included this attention-grabbing nugget:

It is commonly said that TED attendees are every bit as remarkable as those appearing on stage. It happens to be true. That's why at every conference we invite you to consider whether you have something to contribute to the program—and possibly later to the wider TED community, through the TED.com site.

So there at my laptop I raised my virtual hand—so to speak—and submitted a pitch for a three-minute talk to TED. These are the palate cleansers in between the more heady and often very emotional eighteen-minute TED talks. I figured I'd better get right to the pitch. Here's what I wrote:

> The tale of Mister Splashy Pants: a lesson for nonprofits on the Internet. How Greenpeace took itself a little less seriously and helped start an Internet meme that actually got the Japanese government to call off that year's humpback whaling expedition. People manage to sell entire books on the subject of "new media marketing" but I only need three minutes— with the help of this whale—to explain the "secret."

How could they resist a name like Mister Splashy Pants? Splashy to his friends.

I figured they must've been totally floored with awe, because I didn't hear back for a month. Was this just their way of saying no? I was already in India at this point, so I sent a quick "ping" e-mail to see if I could get a yes or no.

"Congratulations. You did get accepted."

Hot damn, I had twenty-four hours to write and rehearse a talk people practice for months....

Better turn on some *South Park*.

Thanks to VPN, I could watch *South Park* from south India. The episode was called "Whale Whores" (season 13, episode 11), and it satirized the Animal Planet documentary-style reality show called *Whale Wars* (oh, puns!), which features the Sea Shepherd Conservation Society, an organization that harasses Japanese whalers in an effort to protect marine life.

In the episode, after hordes of Japanese storm the Denver aquarium during Stan's birthday and slaughter all the dolphins (am I really writing about *South Park* right now? I love this country), an enraged Stan implores his friends to join him in protecting the dolphins and whales, which the Japanese seem so intent on eradicating.

Stan's friends are not interested until Stan joins the cast of *Whale Wars*, at which point Cartman and Kenny pretend to be whale-loving activists in order to milk some of the fame associated with the show. They volunteer, despite admitting earlier that they "don't give two shits about stupid-ass whales."

I grabbed a screen capture of Cartman, in a SAVE THE WHALES shirt, proclaiming his love of whales; Kenny is beside him, DOLPhIN LOVER (*sic*) scrawled on his chest.

That image reminded me of what was then one of the biggest events on reddit—voting for the name for a humpback whale that Greenpeace was tracking. This event has since been eclipsed by other events, such as the "money bomb" donation of over half a million dollars to DonorsChoose .org or fund-raising for three-year-old Lucas Gonzalez, who needed a bone marrow transplant. But the story of Mister Splashy Pants was a special moment in reddit's development and proved to be a prophetic tale of the power of social media: for an idea to truly become mainstream, it needs to go beyond the early adopters—in this case, whale lovers like Stan—and also include those who want to join the trend.

A lot of people rag on PowerPoint (often rightfully so). But in the right hands, this much-maligned communication tool can actually be incredibly entertaining (and even informative). The problem is, most people don't understand how to use it, which sets the bar for PowerPoint presentations *really* low. Here's my philosophy: lots of big pictures, text, and tons of slides. For my TED talk, I had room for no more than a few words on each slide—and they had to be in 86-point type, minimum. Forty-two slides—a good sign,[3] even though it meant I had only a little more than four seconds for each slide.

There was going to be a giant TED sign on the stage behind me. This could make or break my public speaking career. And I was going to be on the same stage where the brilliant statistician Hans Rosling, using beautiful data, emphatically demonstrated how India ascended to economic superpower status—meanwhile, I was going to talk about a whale named Mister Splashy Pants. No pressure.

I finished before sunrise and took a power nap. When I awoke I began feverishly practicing with my timer. I missed all the morning talks. I was terrified of Chris Anderson, who famously cuts off speakers when they go on too long. As someone who routinely talks more than I should, I didn't want my talk punctuated by a giant cane pulling me offstage.

I'd later learn that TED does not in fact use a giant cane.

---

3. *Nerd!* It's the meaning of life, of course. Confused? Read *The Hitchhiker's Guide to the Galaxy.* You're welcome.

I don't remember the talk before mine, because I was so busy trying to remember what I was going to say.

Why are my hands shaking?

Chris Anderson introduced me as Alex. I hate being called Alex, but I smiled and took the stage, trying hard not to trip on the way. When you've grown up embracing your unisex name (okay, it's predominantly a woman's name here in the United States), it's incredibly vexing to hear someone shorten it to the male version. I'm a dude named Alexis; please call me by my name. Now I was thinking about Alexis Argüello, the three-time world champion boxer my father named me after, and I wondered if he ever had the same issue growing up in Nicaragua—shit, I'm supposed to give a talk right now.

Remember, it can't go worse than a giant room of CompUSA shoppers actively ignoring you.

That got me started. Get to it, Ohanian.

"There are a lot of 'Web 2.0 consultants' [I made air quotes with my fingers] who make a lot of money—in fact, they make their livings on this kind of stuff. I'm going to try and save you all the time and all the money and go through it in the next three minutes, so bear with me."

I breathlessly shared the story of Greenpeace's dogged efforts to raise online awareness of their effort to stop Japanese humpback whaling expeditions. They wanted to track one particular whale on its migration and humanize it with a name chosen by their online community. Greenpeace staff chose about twenty very erudite names—like Talei and Kaimana (which means "divine power of the ocean" in a Polynesian language)—and then there was Mister. Splashy. Pants.

I enunciated each word one at a time for full comedic effect. Laughter. They're not hating this.

Once a reddit user discovered the poll and submitted it to reddit.com, a surge of votes flooded in for this obvious favorite. Who doesn't want to hear a news anchor say "Mister Splashy Pants"?

Greenpeace wasn't pleased. They insisted on rerunning the voting process, which only galvanized us. I changed our reddit logo from a smiling whale to a more combative version. For any scientists reading this:

Humpback Whale
(Megaptera novaeangliae)

Fightin' Splashy
(Pugnans splashy)

Breadpig
(Panis porcus)

This time, polls closed with Splashy having an even more commanding lead.

Oh no, I'm running out of time. Please let them be gentle.

Eventually they relented and let the online favorite win (sometimes you just have to let yourself be disrupted, remember), but at this point they'd inadvertently created a brand that excited far more people than just Greenpeace fans—the message had spread far beyond whale lovers. In fact, the Japanese government actually *called off the whaling expedition.*

Everyone who creates something online has lost control of their message but in the process has gained access to a global audience. Mister Splashy Pants is a story about the democratization of content online—starring a whale—and it demonstrated how little control we have over our brands. It turns out we never had control, only now we realize it. Before the social web, we had little idea of what people actually thought about us—now we know, and when like-minded people band together, they wield a really big stick.

The talk is over. Applause. Even a few "Woo!"s from the crowd.

Nailed it. I'd given a few non-CompUSA talks before then, but once the video of my TED talk hit a million views and was front-paged on reddit,[4] I became a known "public speaker."

I have a lecture agent now and get paid more for a speaking gig than I did for an entire year's work at Pizza Hut. It's a little bit insane, but then I remember that I'm still getting paid less than Snooki,[5] which makes me really question things.

I still get nervous before I get onstage—I just know how to better handle the nerves now. In truth, it really is all about practice. Once you've been onstage enough times and make sure you're always well rehearsed and armed with the feeling that you really *know* what you're talking about, it then becomes all about polish. Listen to yourself. I listen (not watch; I want to focus on the words) to every talk I give once afterward to see where the "ums" and "you knows" crept in. I'll pay attention to jokes that didn't work and others that

---

4. In a brilliant illustration of my argument, the video was submitted to reddit with the following headline: "Nutjob mistakenly allowed to give TED Talk, he rambles for over four minutes before being carried off the stage."

5. This is a cultural reference from the early twenty-first century. Readers in the mid-twenty-first century and beyond will probably know her as President Snooki. I mean no disrespect.

worked better than expected—was it the joke or the delivery? Then I put that talk out of mind. Test, analyze, and repeat.

The Internet offers a wealth of great speeches, all freely available with just a few keystrokes. Find your favorite speakers and study them. I notice the way Jon Stewart disarms an interview subject with a joke before hitting him with a knockout punch. President Obama really knows how to hit the Pause button at the right moment for maximum impact. When used well, silence is powerful. And when I learned that Louis C.K.—easily one of the best comics of our generation—trashes all his material every year and starts anew,[6] I knew I needed to keep from getting lazy and recycling entire talks. Louis does it because, he says, "The way to improve is to reject everything you're doing. You have to create a void by destroying everything; you have to kill it. Or else you'll tell the same fucking jokes every night."

Being a stand-up comic is infinitely harder than giving a talk or a speech, so if he can stay that on top of his game, why can't I?

There Are Much Harder Things in Life Than Being an Entrepreneur

Growing up, I had the words LIVES REMAINING: 0 written on the wall of my room. If life were a video game, that's how it'd indicate this is the only chance left.

I'm lucky because I got that lesson when I was twenty-

---

6. http://www.huffingtonpost.com/2011/08/02/louis-ck-just-for-laughs -throw-out-jokes_n_916250.html

two years old and just a month or so out of college, feeling about as immortal as someone could.

But then everything changed with a phone call.

Why's Mom calling me? She should be getting ready for her vacation trip to Norway.

She's crying.

Max, our wonderful mutt, had to be put down.

Because I'm an only child, Max became my mother's favorite when I left home for college—a position in her heart I could never reclaim. She absolutely adored him, and our family did everything we could to help him fight the Cushing's disease that had finally taken its toll.

My mother was understandably distraught. I told her I loved her. I understood why she had to do what she did to our beloved dog and, although it didn't work out that I could be there, I was grateful that she was. She had some more errands to run before meeting up with Dad and heading to the airport. She'd try to get through them the best she could, but I knew it was going to be hard for her to go on vacation.

At least it happened before she got on the plane.

My dog had just died. It was going to be a rough day in Boston. Startup life is extreme enough—every morning one wakes up thinking today's the day you're conquering the world—or today's the day you're doomed.

I got through that awful morning. I don't remember what I was doing at the time, but my phone started buzzing again in the late afternoon.

Why's Dad calling me? He should be at cruising altitude with Mom.

They're in the hospital.

Howard County General.

On any other night Mom would be working there; she'd been a pharmacy technician there on the night shift for the last seventeen years.

Now she was missing the vacation she and my dad had planned for years.

She'd had a seizure in the dressing room of a department store, and an attentive clerk had called 911.

At least it happened before she got on the plane.

The initial brain scans revealed a tumor. The culprit in her skull was an insidious monster called *glioblastoma multiforme*. Such an ugly name. They were going to keep her overnight for more tests. She'd likely have surgery soon thereafter. I never should have done the Google search, but I needed to know what my parents would inevitably struggle to tell me.

I bought a ticket for a flight down first thing the next morning, but until then I was stuck in Boston.

That night Steve and I tried to get our minds off things and went down to a local bar to watch our favorite team play their archrivals on *Monday Night Football*. Our Washington Redskins versus the Dallas Cowboys.

It was a really boring game. And we were losing it. So much for even a brief respite from the shittiest day of my life.

By the fourth quarter, there weren't many TVs with the game still on (we were in Boston, after all). Back in Columbia, Maryland, my dad had already called it a night. He didn't need any more heartache.

Steve and I had nowhere else to go and needed distraction—any distraction—so we kept watching. It was fourth and fifteen, and we were down 13-0 with less than four minutes left (non-football fans: just know that this means an exceptionally dire situation). Just then, Mark Brunell, a quarterback not known for his arm strength, hurled the ball downfield more than fifty yards to Santana Moss in the end zone.

It was 13-6!

But no one on the field was celebrating—and with good reason. There was hardly any time left, and we were still losing. Even the Cowboys' mascot was taunting us with a dramatic look at his wrist to remind us that there wasn't enough time left for our touchdown to matter.

But Steve and I kept cheering. What the hell. They had finally given us something to cheer about. That was our first touchdown of the season! And we'd been drinking, which always helps. We made the extra point, and it was almost a ball game. But that jerk in the Cowboys costume had a point.

Dallas ended up punting quickly, thanks to a stingy Skins defense, and we had the ball again (football novices: that's our time to go on offense and score points).

First and ten from our own thirty-yard line. One of the commentators, John Madden, couldn't even finish his run-on sentence before Brunell threw the *exact same pass* fifty-plus yards down the field right back to Moss, who again beat the coverage.

"And Santana Moss for a touchdown! Wow!" Al Michaels couldn't believe his eyes as Moss hustled into the end zone.

At this point Steve and I were screaming. We were also the only two people still watching the game, I think.

Suddenly it was 14-13 and we were winning.

Winning? What?

Even when all hope seemed lost—see what happened there?—we had to keep hoping, because that was all we had. As much as I wish I could affect the outcome of sporting events from my seat, there's nothing I can do but cheer at the right times.

But it wasn't over. Life isn't a storybook. And what happened next is going to be exceptionally difficult to describe for non-football fans.

The Cowboys weren't about to be upset so spectacularly in their own house on national TV. They briskly marched down the field, nearing field-goal range as the time kept ticking down. They didn't need to reach the end zone; they needed to get just thirty-five yards or so from it. As long as they could kick a field goal, they could walk off the field as victors and dash our hopes.

They were that close, but only for a second.

A third-down completion to Patrick Crayton secured a first down and also put the Cowboys in field-goal range. Crayton got a step beyond the marker and then...contact.

BOOM!

You could hear the pop on the television broadcast.

Sean Taylor, a lean and hungry safety, delivered a brutal—and legal—tackle that popped the ball loose, resulting in an incomplete pass.

BOOM!

I started yelling. Spilling beer. Probably also spitting a little. It was obnoxious because they kept replaying that hit and I kept yelling *BOOM!* louder with every replay.

Steve was yelling, too. Everyone else in the bar was hating us. We didn't give a damn.

Later, I got my hands on the high-def footage of Taylor during and after that hit. He pops up, electrified. That fire. That heart. It's something awesome when you watch a human—just another carbon-based life-form—doing what he does so well. And loving it.

That hit took all the air out of Cowboys Stadium, from the fans to the field. The Cowboys turned the ball over on downs, and Redskins players poured Gatorade on Coach Gibbs. Not a typical week-two celebration, but we thought it was appropriate.

Steve and I went home singing our fight song, and I had the joy of surprising my dad with the news the next morning. He'd never walked out on a game before and never would again.

I don't believe in signs, mostly because I don't think I'm worth all the trouble. But I was inspired.

Sean Taylor saved the day that night, doing what he loved and doing what he was so clearly talented at. It gave me a little bit of happiness on the saddest night of my life and confirmed that it's never over until it's over.

So I'd better not give up. And if I can find something I'm good at and love doing, I'm going to put everything I have into it.

Sean Taylor died two years later. He was shot by an intruder while at home with his girlfriend and daughter. He was twenty-four; just a few weeks older than I was at the time.

We often use words like *bipolar* and *all-consuming* to describe startup life. Fools compare it to combat, and over drinks even the more reasonable among us still veer into hyperbole about how hard it is to face the day some mornings. I've never lain in bed in self-pity, though. Even after that night I didn't, because I knew back in Maryland my mother and father were dealing with a very different kind of morning. Perspective. My mom, the kindest person on earth, had been told she would die before seeing her grandchildren, and yet the first words out of her mouth when she saw me were "I'm sorry."

That's the kind of person she was. I knew I'd lived a rather stress-free life until that point, and I knew that that would have to change. I just didn't think it'd happen all at once.

My mom came to this country when she was twenty-three because she was in love with my dad. After a few years of living together while she was still an undocumented alien, they secretly married at City Hall in lower Manhattan, and only later did they have the "public" wedding for their families (surprise, Grandpa!). Eventually the cost of trying to raise a child in New York City (even in the boroughs—Brooklyn and then Queens) proved to be too much, and my parents moved to the suburbs of Maryland, where my dad's modest income could go much further.

My father had a degree in urban studies and architecture from Antioch College, and my mother wound up getting her GED in 1980, just three years before I was born. She went on to work night shifts as a pharmacy technician, sleeping only a little so she could be present for more of my waking hours.

After all that, my mother—who had supported me my entire life, filled me with confidence, and loved me dearly—was telling me she was sorry she'd inconvenienced *me* by getting terminal brain cancer because it was something else *I'd* have to deal with?

Being an entrepreneur was the best decision I could've made, because not having a boss gave me the freedom to make my family a priority without compromising my work. I got a lot of use out of that 3G USB stick and laptop. As long as I had those two things, I was in the office, whether it was bedside at Hopkins or in the reddit headquarters in Somerville.

I write this all as a precursor to my story—to hell with chronological order—because as empowering as the Internet is (and boy, is it empowering), we must all still succumb to a common mortality.[7] I would trade anything to have my mom back, but in lieu of that, I can only work to honor her a little bit more every day.

To be reading this book, thinking about how to use this great platform, the Internet, to share your world-changing ideas, ideally from a comfortable seat somewhere, is itself a great luxury. We're living in a time of unprecedented opportunity across the globe that happens to coincide with a time of tremendous misfortune.

Let's make the most out of this great hand we've been dealt, eh?

---

7. Except for the sentient robots. They're going to be fine. Don't shed a tear for them, because they wouldn't for you—and they can't; that'd be a lot of needless engineering.

CHAPTER TWO

The Story of reddit from College to Condé Nast

We hold these truths to be self-evident, that all men are created equal, that they are endowed by their Creator with certain unalienable Rights, that among these are Life, Liberty and the pursuit of Happiness.

Thomas Jefferson, United States
Declaration of Independence

Jefferson's vision is taking a bit longer than expected to become a reality. The American dream is rooted in a country where anyone with enough talent and enough determination can accomplish whatever she or he wants. Unfortunately, we're not there yet, but a pair of undergraduates at the University of Virginia once got lucky on spring break during their senior year, inadvertently playing a small part in the reboot of that dream, at least on the Internet. The dream that motivates people to create something online isn't limited to a single nationality—America's dream, while still very much a work in progress in this country, is largely a reality on the global World Wide Web. My own part in that story started when I met Steve Huffman, realized how much I liked waffles, and started building the front page of the Internet.

When we left off in chapter 1, Steve and I had just met. We spent most of our free time together in college playing video games or pranks on one another (I ended up on the receiving end most of the time). I'd had ambitions to study computer science because of how much I enjoyed it during high school, but that all changed once I met people like Steve and realized I'd better nurture my computer talents as a hobby only. I became a history major and told myself I was going to study law and become an immigration lawyer. I suddenly became an overachiever who cared too much about his GPA because I knew, as an out-of-state student, that my parents wouldn't have been able to afford UVA if it weren't for a generous gift from my great-aunt Vera (great *and* great, for which I'm endlessly grateful). She made sure I never had to take out a student loan, and for that reason I wanted to get the most out of my four years—that's why I majored in history and business (graduating with high honors) and minored in German.

By my junior year, however, I realized I didn't want to be a lawyer. This epiphany came while I was with my friend Jack Thorman at a Waffle House, which I highly recommend for both the epiphanies and the waffles. Steve had already gotten a job offer from a small software company in Virginia. I myself had waffled (puns!) about becoming an immigration lawyer until I'd realized that Saturday mornings are better spent enjoying breakfast. At that point I abruptly walked out of the Kaplan LSAT prep course I was taking.

Something happened in between those syrupy bites; I

needed to know why I had wanted to spend three very expensive years getting a piece of paper that would make me a lawyer. In truth, I didn't *know*. Steve and I had had far too many great brainstorming sessions over beer and pizza for me to give up on turning one of those ideas into a reality.

One of these discussions started because Steve hated having to wait while he finished pumping his gas at Sheetz before going inside to order his sub. They'd already made ordering more efficient by using touch screens at the counter, but why not take the order before that, via mobile phone? As Steve told me this I thought about all the implications mobile food ordering would have for *any* take-out order you'd normally wait in line for. You're going to get the same Frappuccino you always get, so why not place the order with a couple of clicks so it'll be ready when you walk in? This just might work, Steve....

The previous year, I'd spent a formative summer in Singapore, competing on behalf of UVA at an international technopreneurship conference (oh, bless the Singaporeans and their technopreneurship conferences). One of my favorite teachers, Professor Mark White, had invited me to go on this all-expenses-paid trip. I'd even turned down an internship at Ogilvy because I like free travel even more than I like unpaid internships in the most expensive city in America. It was there in Singapore on our first night that I pitched Mark the idea Steve and I had cooked up. Mark's was the first unbiased feedback I'd gotten on the idea (my parents had always been ludicrously supportive of whatever I told them I was up to), and he thought we'd be able to pull it off.

His optimism may've just been a combination of the jet lag and the Singapore slings, but I was thrilled.

I wrote Steve this e-mail the very next morning. It's in its original form for authenticity. Please forgive all the typos; those keyboards in Singapore aren't QWERTY. Apparently there's also a button on those keyboards that keeps inserting "bro" everywhere—sorry about that. In fact, imagine a great big [sic] around this whole thing:

> hey bro, i'm in singapore at this technepreneurial seminar, and am basically spending a week learning how to create a tech startup. i spoke to Mark White (a professor in the comm school, the guy who took me to South Africa, and who recruited me to come here, as well as a generally good guy and technophile) over some drinks last nite, and pitched him on our idea…from his feedback—and let me remind you that he gets pitches every couple of months from students, and was very candid and honest with his thoughts, but basically said it was one of the best he's heard, period. Not only that, but he wants to be on the board of directors, and already knows some people to hit up for starting capital…I've got plenty of more details, but I am seriously considering putting off law school for this, but i need you, and we'll both need to be doing this full time for about a year to get it off the ground…but the potential he saw was in the millions my friend…we need to talkseriously.i am coming back the 20th so if we could have lunch around 1pm i could meet you whereever you'd like…let me know.honestly, this is the kind of thing that could change our lives—and his motivation has really spurred me.but i need you and the same kind of commitment.

How could he say no? Well, he didn't quite say yes, but I was starting to wear Steve down.

I asked my commercial law professor (the same one who praised me for always taking the initiative) to recommend a lawyer in town, and we got our first company, Redbrick Solutions, LLC, registered in the commonwealth of Virginia with Steve and me as co-founders. Then I set up a bank account with the Bank of America branch that four years earlier had given me my first ATM card. It was around this time I realized I'd better sign up for the well-known entrepreneurship class (COMM 468) that the McIntire School of Commerce offered only in the spring to fourth-year students.

The Time I Wasn't Allowed into the Entrepreneurship Class

That was a bit of a spoiler, I know, but you'll want to hear why.

COMM 468: Entrepreneurship was a popular class, and the best I could do was secure a spot on the waiting list posted outside the professor's door. I wasn't exactly first on the list, but I figured I had a pretty good case, given that I was already committed to entrepreneurship—after all, I'd already incorporated with my co-founder and established a bank account. I think I'd even designed business cards.

In short: this wasn't going to be a classroom hypothetical; this was my life.

Unfortunately, I learned from Professor Brockett, who'd be teaching the class that semester, that we were required to work on our "business plan" with another pair of students. If only I'd known then what a recipe for failure four co-founders usually is, I could've said something at that point, but the bigger issue to me and Steve back then was that we weren't in a position to add two random co-founders to our very real business.

From: Alexis Ohanian
Sent: Tue 1/25/2005 7:46 a.m.
To: Brockett, Tanya
Subject: Interested in auditing COMM 468 for this spring
Professor Brockett,

[...] I do hope you consider allowing me to audit this class, because I know how much I'll be referring to my notes and thinking back on lectures when May comes around. We plan on hitting the ground running once the semester ends, but despite all the administrative tasks I <think> I've already completed, I know others will pop up—and I'd like to be as prepared as possible. I've already read a number of books and have drawn from the advice of some McIntire faculty with regard to starting this business—so there shouldn't be any doubts about my interest in the subject.

However, Steve and I had our weekly progress meeting last night, and we really wouldn't feel too comfortable with developing a business plan with a pair of other students. Firstly because we've already made one, but secondly because we still haven't finished the software and therefore can't protect it.

Despite the fact that I need 3 credits of a 400-level management class to graduate (and that I'm already taking 18 this semester)—I feel confident that I can course action into another management class, assuming I audited this one. I can assure you my presence will only add value to the class, and if there is any question to whether or not I could handle 21 credit hours—I took 22 last spring.

Thanks for taking my request into consideration,

Alexis

That e-mail was way longer than it needed to be, but I figured it would do the trick. At least I cut down on the "bro's" this time.[1]

Here's what Professor Brockett told me, with my thoughts in *italics*:

Alexis,

Your position on the waitlist did allow you to win a seat in class.

HUZZAH! It worked. I knew she'd see the importance of this class for me....

However, you have not yet been added because we need to clarify the expectations given your last email.

Ugh. My great-aunt is paying out-of-state tuition for this?

Please contact me during office hours (4:00–5:30; I already have a 3:30 appt) on Wednesday the 26th so we can discuss this.

---

1. In the early 2000s, keyboards often had a Bro Lock button that was even more pointless than Caps Lock—by then I'd learned how to turn it off.

Fail sauce.

I called Professor Brockett, who told me that I could work on a new business plan with three other students. So I asked about auditing the class, but she told me no.

And that's how I was thwarted from taking COMM 468: Entrepreneurship. I opted to just be an entrepreneur instead.

Acceptance, Rejection, and Reacceptance; or Places to Drink in Harvard Square

I continued "entrepreneuring" during my senior year. Steve and I pushed on with our idea, and I began talking to local restaurateurs about their point-of-sale systems and experiences using online ordering, which back then was basically a glorified fax service. I was learning a lot, and all indications were that we'd stay in Charlottesville after we graduated to build our company: My Mobile Menu (MMM!).

Our lives changed with a fateful trip to Cambridge that spring of our senior year. One of Steve's idols, Paul Graham, announced he'd be speaking at Harvard, and Steve's girlfriend suggested he go. When he sent me the link, I responded with gusto (despite not really knowing who Graham was) because I'd never been to Boston and the theme sounded perfect for us: "How to Start a Startup."

Granted, it was during our spring break, but it's not like we were going to the beach anyway. The sun makes using a laptop nearly impossible, the screen glare is terrible, and besides, there's all that sand.

Graham had started a company called Viaweb—the first online store—during the first dot-com bubble. He sold it for fifty million dollars to Yahoo!, which gave him the financial security to focus on his art and publish essays online about all things having to do with startups and programming. By the early aughts, he'd become a pundit in the tech community with a significant following of programmers, including Steve.

I didn't expect there to be so much snow. We'd taken an agonizingly long train ride up from Virginia, spent our first night at a friend's apartment, and prepared for the talk. Actually, Steve leveled up his priest in World of Warcraft.[2]

But then we were off to Harvard! The lecture room was packed, and Paul read from his notes for about forty-five minutes and graciously answered questions. At one moment he described the perfect angel investors as "people who themselves got rich from technology." As he said this, he must've noticed the roomful of aspiring founders all widen their eyes with hopefulness. He abruptly clarified: "Oh, not me!"

The rumble of one hundred simultaneously disappointed nerds echoed through the room.

Graham would look back on this moment as the instant he realized a little money could go a long way for the right founders. After all, he'd just told them, "You need three things to create a successful startup: to start with good people, to make something customers actually want, and to spend as little money as possible. Most startups that fail do it because they fail at one of these. A startup that does all three will probably succeed."[3]

---

2. I hadn't yet fallen victim to WoW because I'd gone through it all before with EverQuest. As a bard, no less.

3. http://www.paulgraham.com/start.html

After he finished, Steve made a beeline for him to get an autograph, and I followed. When it was my turn, I informed him that we'd come all the way from Virginia and said (rather boldly), "It'd totally be worth the cost of buying you a drink to get your opinion of our startup."

He agreed, probably impressed by our pilgrimage, set a time for the meeting, and asked if I knew "the kiosk." We'd meet there.

I was so excited that I nodded without thinking. Of course, I had no idea where "the kiosk" was, but that didn't stop me from dancing a quick jig in the hallway. After asking a good half dozen strangers, we learned it was, in fact, just a kiosk in the middle of Harvard Square. There's one more reason I didn't go to Harvard.

We met Paul that night as planned and sat down for coffee at Café Algiers to discuss our idea. The plan had been that Steve would impress him with his programming acumen and, once we'd established our competence, I'd slide in with the pitch. Instead, Paul just looked at me and said, "Let's hear it." I didn't get more than a few sentences in.

Paul loved it. Steve still fondly remembers this as an awesome moment of validation. Here was one of his heroes saying that the idea we'd had to start a company wasn't awful. In fact, he said we had a pretty good shot at making it work. I don't remember the odds he gave us, but they reinforced our belief that we'd made the right choice. I know I was relieved, since it was me who was dragging Steve away from a well-paying job at a company he liked. I didn't want to deal with the wrath of his mom if things went poorly, either. We left behind our frozen geeky spring break and returned to Charlottesville enthusiastic about our prospects. I asked Steve to send a follow-up e-mail to Paul, since he was his idol, after all, and it seemed prudent to at least thank him for his time.

A day or so passed, and Steve still hadn't written it, so I literally stood behind him as he typed out a quick e-mail thanking Paul. Steve reminded him that we were "those college students from Virginia." Paul responded within a couple of hours. This was a very good sign. He noted that he was thinking of starting a program to invest in early-stage founders like us and that since he'd already met us, we had a pretty good shot at getting in.

Then, a few weeks later, Paul announced Y Combinator, an experiment in seed-stage investing. The premise was simple: a little bit of money, guidance, and three intensive months of writing code and talking to users could one day result in a billion-dollar company. Granted, at the end of three months, the goal was just to have gotten far enough to raise another round of funding—an angel investment, typically a few hundred thousand dollars. The angels, or backers, would invest in unproven Internet entrepreneurs because so little money is required to start a website—especially compared to how expensive it was when Paul Graham did it. If the founders could feed and house themselves and pay for laptops and Internet, they could launch a startup.

We applied for the very first round of Y Combinator funding and were invited up to Boston for an interview on Saturday, April 9, 2005. Jessica Livingston, partner at YC, described the interview process in an e-mail:

At this stage we believe you are technically capable, so we plan to spend the allotted 40 minutes[4] discussing your idea. We don't want you to give a presentation, but please come prepared to talk about:

1) Why your idea is something that people will want

2) How you will sell it to customers

3) How you will do this better than your competitors

This was a tremendous change from most tech-related interviews. There were no thought exercises like "Why are manholes round?" or stress tests with yelling and "big swinging dicks"[5]—they wanted to see us at our best, not flustered. Jessica greeted us at the door with a smile. When our time came, we had a lively discussion with Paul and his partners at the table: Jessica, Robert Morris, and Trevor Blackwell. Once it was all done, we still felt pretty good about our odds. He'd been so excited for our startup just a month earlier.

Getting the rejection call from Paul that night wasn't easy. Steve and I dealt with it as best as we could, telling one another we'd prove Y Combinator wrong.

exhibit (A)
how Steve & I felt, in breadpig form

---

4. You can tell we were in the first "class" of funding applicants. Because there are so many people seeking funding, Y Combinator partners offer little more than ten minutes during these interviews nowadays.

5. This is a metaphor. Thankfully. I first encountered it in the book *Liar's Poker*, by Michael Lewis.

Fortunately, there was a cure for our disappointment: beer.

exhibit (B)
how Steve & I felt, four hours later

After doing some damage at the Border Cafe in Harvard Square, we went out with the pal who was putting us up. He was a Harvard graduate and took us to one of the scenes frequented by final club members (read: Harvard frat guys). I distinctly remember being introduced to some successful alums who were talking about finance jobs. They asked what we were doing with our lives. Drunkenly, I said something about how we were in town fund-raising for our startup and had just gotten funding from this new firm called Y Combinator.

Ugh. I felt so dirty when the words came out of my mouth, but I was so ashamed I couldn't bring myself to admit our failure out loud. They weren't even impressed; for some reason I thought they would be. Never again. The conversation had drifted back to something else, probably the girls in the bar they were eyeing, and I staggered outside for some air. I love being outside at night—maybe it's the lack of sunlight, but I was really disappointed with myself. (Hey, if you Harvard alums from that night are reading this, I was lying because I was so embarrassed about being rejected by Y Combinator—I grew up in the generation of kids who got trophies for everything, so the first big rejection in my life really, really sucked.)

I had to accept it. We were rejected. And I was going to do everything I could to prove them wrong. Steve and I would show them that we didn't need to be in their summer camp for startups. We'd go back down to Charlottesville and work with renewed vigor on an idea that would change the world—once we recovered from our hangovers.

Then everything changed with a phone call. Don't worry; it's much better than the calls I got in chapter 1.

Somewhere in the middle of Connecticut, on an exceptionally long train ride back to Virginia, my cell phone rang. It was Paul Graham. He wanted us back, but only if we changed our idea to something else.[6] So much for proving them wrong. We got off at the very next stop, but not before I got Paul to buy us a pair of tickets to fly back to Charlottesville that night so we could return to Boston for an hour to join him in brainstorming a better idea than mobile food ordering. The big problem with the concept was that not only did we have to persuade customers to use the product, but because this was a time before app stores, the only way to get our software on people's phones was to make deals with mobile carriers first. That alone would've been an impressive feat for a brand-new company of two, but we'd also need to get restaurateurs—notoriously late adopters—on board as well. Yikes.

We got back to the Y Combinator office and met with

---

6. We would later learn that Jessica Livingston was the partner who saved us. She thought we, particularly Steve, were too endearing to reject. Most YC founding teams get a nickname among the partners; ours was "the muffins." Thanks, Jessica.

Paul Graham alone, without his partners. He told us to forget mobile for a moment and consider building something for the browser. Long before most people realized the power of online software, he knew the Internet offered tremendous potential for an idea to spread as never before. When a customer only needs a browser and an Internet connection to access your product, unprecedented growth is possible. He asked us about frustrations we had using the Internet, which had just recently seen the launch of a college-only site called TheFacebook.com. Steve was an avid reader of Slashdot, a news website with editorial oversight and a robust community of commenters as well as a moderation system. I had too many tabs open every day—they showed me a range of news websites, but I had no way to filter signal from noise. At the time, a website called del.icio.us (pronounced "delicious"; ignore the dots) let people bookmark websites online, so if you hopped between computers, your reference material followed you. An interesting by-product of this was del.icio.us/popular, which aggregated the most popular bookmarked URLs at any given time. There was something here that del.icio.us wasn't quite getting, but we saw the potential for something bigger, which would sort not the most popular links for bookmarking but the most popular links for sharing.

We hadn't figured out functionality, but we knew the old model for news aggregation, when it was printed on a dead tree, wasn't suited for the Internet age. In fact, the vision was best crystallized by Paul Graham in that very meeting: "That's it! You should build the front page of the web."

Early Decisions

Once we were accepted into Y Combinator, we got back to studying for finals and enjoying our last weeks of college.

On 4/14/05, Steve Huffman wrote:
Paul said it would be nice to whip up a prototype. We don't need to make anything work, but a quick page to show what our site might look like could be cool. Do you have any time this weekend?
    Steve

To which I responded:

yeah man,
    sat afternoon or sunday—all day sunday would work well. i have some ideas, but i'll need to sit down and sketch some things out with ya.

                                                    -alexis

There it is. Were you expecting something more dramatic? Two college seniors just agreeing to get together over their laptops one weekend. That's how mundane starting a top-fifty website is. There's no parting of clouds or springing from foreheads—just deciding to set aside some time on a Sunday to get some work done.

We did start thinking about reddit a bit, although I didn't come up with the name until a couple of weeks later. I promptly registered it on April 29, just a few days after my twenty-second birthday.

After graduation, Steve and I started working in earnest in a rented apartment in Medford, Massachusetts, a quiet neighborhood outside Cambridge. I'd found the place, which was subleased by some Tufts students, on craigslist; all I knew was that it needed to be on the MBTA Red Line and it had to be cheap. We'd shown up with a month's worth of clothes (it was already furnished), our laptops, and some sketches in our notebooks, including one of the logo and one of our alien mascot (in truth, I'd created these months before we'd even figured out how the site would work. Priorities!).

Steve and I set out that June to build a website where readers, not editors, would determine the front page of what's new and interesting by submitting links to be voted on by the community. We had no ambitions to have the president of the United States conduct a real-time interview with millions of people on our site, which he would end up doing—from Charlottesville, no less—seven years later; we just wanted to create a place where anyone at any time could find what was new and interesting online. These could be links to an article, a video, or even a photo of a cat; if users like it, they vote it up (and vote it down if they don't). Neologisms like *upvote* and *downvote* came into existence without any forethought—I just liked the way an up-and-down arrow looked.

The first version of the site used two words a user could click on, *interesting* and *boring*. We even debated dropping the "negative vote"—whatever it'd end up being called or looking like—in favor of a binary "I like this!" button, perhaps in the shape of a star. Fortunately, we'd already had a taste for how good it felt to bring a bit of retribution to the submitter of a bad link with a click of the downvote button, so it stayed and I got back to redesigning exactly how those arrows should look—down to the pixel.

We didn't anticipate how much people would adore getting these upvotes, but we did know that the karma score (your total upvotes minus your total downvotes) would be a great incentive, especially early on, for people to submit. And when you're trying to build a community from scratch, you need a simple system to encourage participation. The point system was neither novel nor fancy; it just worked. Steve engineered a clever algorithm to keep links rising and falling based on their votes and time, producing constant freshness.

The most pivotal product decision we made seemed much less important at the time but was our first big fight. I really wanted "tags" as a way to categorize content, and Steve insisted we let users launch their own reddits within our network (we'd call them subreddits). Just like WordPress was a blogging platform for online publishing, reddit would be a platform for online communities. It didn't seem important at the time, but Steve was absolutely right and it's a damn good thing he won because that decision would ultimately drive reddit's success where all of our then competitors failed. We combined this simple point system with the ability for anyone to create a forum for an online community to share and discuss links—from NFL fans (/r/NFL) to corgi lovers (/r/corgi).[7] The resulting network is a black hole of productivity worldwide.

We applied essentially the same model to our commenting system, which as a result generates the best discussions on the Internet. We added that commenting system a few months after we launched and I still remember Steve promising "something awesome" as he dashed off to get started building it—boy, did he deliver. I wish more people copied the reddit commenting system so I wouldn't have to question my faith in humanity every time I watch a YouTube video and glance at the comments. But we started, as all startups do, with only ourselves as users.

I came up with the name reddit (as in, "I read it on reddit"[8]) while I was in the Alderman Library at UVA one day, but we didn't settle on it until just a couple of weeks before the launch. It was almost reditt, but fortunately I asked my friend Melissa Goldstein which bastardization made more

---

7. That's not to say these two communities are mutually exclusive. In fact, I'm a proud member of both.

8. I'd hoped people would say this to one another, but to date, I don't think a single person has. So it goes.

"sense." She chose wisely, and I stuck with reddit from then on. Yet it nearly became something else. Thanks, Melissa.

The alternatives we considered back then were even more ridiculous, and plenty of people offered suggestions. I blame domain squatters for making this such a difficult proposition (and, frankly, a waste of time, given there are more important things to do, like building the product). The result was that my in-box became full of e-mails like this one from Steve:

how about oobaloo.com? i like it

Or this one from Paul Graham:

360scope.com. I like this one. A 360scope being something that looks in all directions, rather than a microscope or telescope, which look[s] at either extreme of one direction. You can imagine people saying, let's go check out the 360scope.

Nevertheless, I wasn't changing my mind. I also really wanted a mascot. By the way, I've met a few people who've had the reddit alien tattooed on their bodies, which never ceases to amaze me (and is something I hope they never regret), but the little creature had to win over my co-founder, Steve, and our chief investor, Paul.

From: Paul Graham
Date: June 22, 2005 1:29:10 p.m. EDT
To: Steve Huffman, Alexis Ohanian
Cc: Jessica Livingston
Subject: prototype

Also, get the content as far as you can into the upper left.

That's what people came for. Smoosh the logo and put the login on the right side.

In fact you might want to consider getting rid of the logo....

If you're attached to the little bug guy, put him at the bottom instead of the top; then it looks like a joke instead of branding.

—pg

Needless to say, I didn't heed Paul's advice. He's brilliant, but also a fallible human just like the rest of us. Though Steve waffled a bit on the name, I certainly wasn't going to change it or the mascot. Besides, there were more important discussions we needed to have just then.

Steve and I would have brainstorming sessions with pens and notebooks, which I'd take to PaintShop Pro 5.0 so that I could mock up designs and layouts, sometimes even for random ideas that had no chance of coming to fruition anytime soon. We only had one developer, of course, and that was Steve, who was responsible for everything technical. Thanks to him, those pixels I doodled actually became something useful. Today he's rightly respected as one of the best developers in our industry, but back then he was a fresh computer science major with almost zero experience in developing software for the web. If he'd taken a job at an established software company, it'd more than likely have been at the ground-floor level. Instead he was a CTO, albeit at a company of two. But without a gatekeeper, he was (and we were) able to learn as we went.

Steve's senior thesis was his first substantial chunk of web code. He didn't know anything about databases, user experience design, or scaling, but he'd read enough online that he figured he could just learn it along the way. "Everything I had learned about programming, I'd already learned online. That's the culture of development right now. More than any other piece of knowledge, how to program is on the Internet."[9]

This makes sense: the Internet was built by programmers, so it's no surprise that programmers have made it such a fertile place to learn the trade. Programming also happens to be a field that Steve calls the world's most valuable profession. I totally agree. Not everyone succeeds in mastering it, but it's getting easier and easier to acquire the skills to build things on your own. I'll go into more depth about this in chapter 4, but your search engine is the easiest place to start learning how to write software (for free, right now!) and how to do everything else you'll need to create the next [insert your favorite startup here]. Just wait until this chapter is finished before you go, okay?

Every morning we listened to the hit song of that summer, "Hollaback Girl," by Gwen Stefani. I'm not sure why or how it got started, but it became our morning ritual. Shit was bananas. We didn't go out a lot during those first weeks; instead we played World of Warcraft for recreation. When I hit level 60, which was then the cap in the game, I retired the account to focus on the more pressing quests of startup

---

9. This is from a recorded interview with Steve Huffman.

life. It took about a month of work, day and night—and daily Gwen Stefani—to get something online that was only slightly embarrassing. After all, to paraphrase LinkedIn founder Reid Hoffman, if you're not a little embarrassed by what you've launched, you waited too long. It need only be good enough to be useful. There's no big secret. Just build the simplest possible solution to a real problem. The motto of Y Combinator is this rather obvious, yet immensely valuable, goal: make something people want.

Back in June of 2005, we thought we had something people wanted. What we didn't have was users. When sharing anything you've created with the world, you have to assume at the start that no one gives a damn about it. Well, maybe your mom does (you hope). But everyone else needs to be convinced that what you've made, whatever it is, is worth his or her attention. To quote Paul Graham: "The Back button is your enemy." This simple fact about online creation forces us to make something compelling and to value our audience as much as possible.

So how do you get people to look at your user-driven website when you don't have any users? You fake them, naturally. That's what Steve and I did for the first few weeks—submit content under different user names. Sure, we asked our friends for help, but only a few really committed themselves to helping our nascent venture (thanks, Connor Dolan and Morgan Carey!). Our first surge of traffic that didn't come from browbeaten friends was thanks to an essay Paul Graham wrote, which sent over the first redditors (reddit + editor, since all users have submission and voting privileges) and got us off to a great start. People actually seemed to be using the site. Maybe we'd made something people wanted after all.

The Alien and the Importance of Giving a Damn

Our first milestone came the day Steve and I simply read the site as everyone else did, not faking submissions. Suddenly there were scores of user names we hadn't created. You can be sure we treated those users like gold. That's not to say we locked them in a vault (early attempts were discouraging); rather, we were vigilant about responding to *anyone* who wrote to us about reddit publicly or privately. Say you wrote a brief blog entry about reddit and how much you hated the mascot—fortunately, this didn't happen often. You can bet you would have gotten a comment from me, thanking you for the feedback but gently letting you know that the alien wasn't going anywhere. Don't be afraid to show your users that you give a damn. It should shine in everything you do, from the design of your website to the way you respond to feedback e-mails.

To this day, when I find myself doing something I know a normal person wouldn't do, I know I'm onto something. When you wake up every morning with the privilege of doing something you love, it's easy.

I still remember the first blog that was ever written about reddit. It was called *Changing Way* and was written by a guy named Andrew.[10] He probably didn't have more than a hundred readers a day, but I was thrilled. In what became my routine, I commented on the piece. I tried to comment on

---

10. I found it thanks to the Internet Archive's Wayback Machine! http://web.archive.org/web/20051026085633/http://changingway.net/archives/221

everything I saw written about reddit, good or bad. The legacy of articles mentioning reddit is covered with comments from me thanking the authors for their feedback. I even got Steve to comment on this one, too. Andrew thanked us for stopping by. I wonder if he still uses reddit....

On the first Fourth of July after we launched, I decided to borrow an idea from Google and doodle a special logo for the day. It looked awful.

I hadn't even learned vector graphics; I was still using outdated software from when I was in high school. The result is a less-than-stellar celebration of our nation's birthday, but it was the first of hundreds of doodles I'd draw, sometimes every morning for days in a row. I found it cathartic. In contrast to all the chaos in my personal life, it was consistent and delightful. My mother would talk to me about what the reddit alien was doing every morning when I'd call her. Those 120 × 40 pixels were a canvas for me, a way to make her smile. The users appreciated it, too, but while my art was often inspired by them, it wasn't made for them. It was for me and Mom.

The first time I used my reddit logo doodles to tell a story, it lasted five days—the week leading up to Thanksgiving—and involved five different logos.

It all started so well.

You can probably see where this is going. Did you notice the Pilgrim got a little bit skinnier?

Cornucopias are even harder to draw than they are to spell, especially when you've got such limited real estate.

Looking rather gaunt, an American Indian offers sustenance. A turkey! (Almost our national bird![11])

---

11. http://www.chron.com/life/article/The-turkey-was-almost-our-national-bird-1732163.php

And here's how the Indian's kind gesture would be repaid. The smallpox blankets aren't pictured, but upon reflection, this is quite a statement for a logo doodle. The longest series I did ended up spanning thirty days in a row. An entire month of doodling every morning, usually before I ate, and even *before* I checked my e-mail.

To this day, long-term redditors remind me how much they enjoyed visiting the site in the early days, if only to see what the alien was up to. Granted, we hoped they'd stick around for the great content, but…baby steps. Since I left reddit full-time, our users have restyled logos for the thousands of sub-reddits that flourish on our open platform. Want a subreddit for a community of corgi lovers? Make it! Oh right, actually, one already exists (r/corgi), but there's nothing to stop you from making a better one. No surprise: it has an adorable corgi logo. It's humbling to see all the superior artists who now use our platform and contribute their talents to building communities around this idea of damn-giving.

Magic happens when you give a damn. I used to organize "press tours" for myself—I would send cold e-mails to jour-nalists to say I'd be in town with only an hour or two avail-able to meet with them. I was taking the Fung Wah bus from Boston to New York every month or so and crashing on a friend's sofa while concocting new ways to share our story.

For a period of time I'd find the number one post on reddit

that day and e-mail the person who made the content. I would tell the person the news about hitting number one on reddit and present him or her with a very special award—a gold alien! (Gold is expensive, so I simply attached an image of a gold reddit alien that looked like a trophy and joked about it being suitable for framing.) One of those winners was a *New York Times* journalist whom I'd never met before. He recently wrote me to say: "One of my favorite moments in my seventeen years at the *New York Times* was when you presented me with the reddit Alien. I still keep it among my treasured memories. You and reddit have gone on to great things since then."

As Paul Graham says, you must be "relentlessly resourceful"[12] as a startup because you have so little going for you. Paul isn't one to use football metaphors, but he compares the resourcefulness of good startup founders to that of running backs: "A good running back is not merely determined, but flexible as well. They want to get downfield, but they adapt their plans on the fly." He's right. But I'd go a step further, because great running backs also keep driving their legs forward after contact, which—if you'll permit me—reflects the relentlessness one needs in the face of adversity. You must give more damns than your competition about your technology (as Steve does) and your audience (as I do). If you do, it'll pay off.

Why It Pays to Be Good

It turns out that an entire building full of editors, no matter how smart or tireless they are, can't match the speed or

---

12. http://www.paulgraham.com/relres.html

efficiency with which the reddit communities discover, create, and promote interesting content. This made reddit an extremely valuable destination. Word of mouth did the rest. I never spent more than a few hundred dollars on advertising for reddit. That's not a typo. And I spent that money on stickers. To this day, you can still find them around Boston. But they started out as just a cheap way to thank users. Whether I handed them out at talks or mailed them to users who found bugs, they were all the advertising our company needed to grow. Thank you, Internet.

That was enough to get the attention of Condé Nast, whose head of biz dev, Kourosh Karimkhany, e-mailed me about licensing our software. Then, just sixteen months after Steve and I first showed up in Massachusetts, Condé Nast acquired reddit.com. All in all, we had raised only $82,000 in funding, which essentially paid for our apartment, pasta, and servers. At the time of acquisition (for an undisclosed sum—sorry!), our biggest monthly expense was the fifteen hundred dollars a month we spent on the three-bedroom rental in Somerville. At the time of this writing, reddit is a top-fifty website, with more than sixty-five million unique visitors a month who generate more than four billion page views. In industry speak, that's a metric shit-ton.[13]

Along the way, we experienced an entire book's worth of

---

13. Author's note: If you're reading this at a time when reddit.com has become even more popular, possibly even forming its own online city-state, think of the above as charmingly humble. If instead it's fallen into obscurity, chuckle knowingly at how dated this book is. I wrote this original chapter in cuneiform, after all.

stories, many of which I've chronicled on my blog (Alexis Ohanian.com). There'll you'll also find plenty of photos my editor said would detract from the legitimacy of this text. Now would be a good time to head to your closest Internet-enabled device and peruse the site until you're satiated. I'll be here when you return.

Our success is just one example of many in a world where a pair of twenty-year-olds needn't ask anyone for permission. If you can build it, all it costs is a credit card to cover the server fees, which will be cheaper than your cell phone bill. Tell your parents you need to move in for a couple of months to get your project off the ground. The only advice I can give that I guarantee is true is that you'll never succeed unless you try. Just please start. You don't need anyone's permission—certainly not mine.

CHAPTER THREE

Hipmunk Takes the Agony out of Online Travel Search

It's really hard to design products by focus groups. A lot of times, people don't know what they want until you show it to them.

Steve Jobs[1]

"Adam really wants to call it Suckage, but that won't fly," Steve explains to me as we're discussing the default sort option for our soon-to-launch travel search engine. It's about halfway

---

1. http://www.businessweek.com/1998/21/b3579165.htm

through August in 2010, and I've only been on the team a week. I'm sleeping on Steve's sofa while we work in the living room of our friend and hipmunk co-founder and CEO, Adam Goldstein. The idea for the search engine is simple enough: make sure people get the best flight for their dollar, maximizing suck reduction (a scientific term) by ranking flight search results based on criteria beyond price alone, such as number of stops and flight duration. We're days away from launch, and Steve is browsing through an online thesaurus for various synonyms for *pain* when he comes across it: *agony*.

Agony. *We'll take the agony out of online travel search.*

Words couldn't express how delighted I was. Adam somewhat randomly picked the name of the site after his girlfriend wisely suggested choosing a misspelling of a cute animal (perfect for an Alexis mascot!), and the name hipmunk (*chipmunk* without the *c*) was available at auction for a low price. Though I'd have protested, it could've ended up being called BouncePounce, but the concept of "agony"— and taking it out of travel—was so awesome I don't think Adam or Steve even realized it at the time. We'd stumbled onto the perfect word for branding our delightful alternative to everything in the travel search market. So while Steve built the ultimate product and Adam hustled all the deals that would let us take off, I'd take advantage of every opportunity to build the hipmunk brand.

But first, let's go back a couple of months. Steve first told me about the idea in May via e-mail:

> Basically, we're doing travel search.... It's not too glamorous, but it's a huge market and the big players really suck.

Steve never was a salesman, but he certainly could get to the point.

In San Francisco, I got an early demo of the then-unnamed travel search website. It was a rather unexciting list of search results, just like any other travel search engine you've ever used, except this one didn't have any polish. I wasn't too impressed. But Steve said they'd been noodling on some different ways to present the data that were going to be infinitely more user-friendly. I trusted him, but I went back to Brooklyn thinking he and Adam were a long way from that minimum viable product (or as the cool kids say, "MVP").

In my mind, searching for flights was already a solved problem. It worked well enough to allow me to sit at my laptop and, if I had enough tabs open, not bother my dad about finding me a good flight to San Francisco. But Adam knew it could be so much better. You see, Adam realized he had a problem booking flights back in college. He ended up memorizing airport codes from AAL to ZRH because the MIT debate team competed all over the globe, and Adam had the unenviable job of booking flights for everyone. He absolutely hated it. It was too hard running all those searches, in all those open tabs of his browser, while deciphering hundreds of search results that confounded him with codeshares and tight connections (or ludicrous layovers).

If finding a good flight is this hard for an MIT graduate, what about the rest of us? At first, however, Adam had a hard time persuading other people that it could be any different. This is a common problem for entrepreneurs who try to solve problems people don't realize they have. It's not until you present most people—even me—with a better alternative that they realize how bad things used to be. That's why it's important for the founders of any Internet company to build something so damn useful that everyone wonders how they ever lived without it.

So after Adam graduated, he came to Steve to talk him out of early retirement. Steve, however, was significantly less enthusiastic when he heard the pitch. "I totally agreed that it was a nice company to start because it was close to people's wallets," he told me. "But I *hated* travel. It's an industry that's *so* not startup friendly."

Soon, however, Steve realized that this hostile market was the perfect reason to try disrupting it with smart innovation—because it was so starved of quality solutions. "No one was thinking about what consumers really want," Steve said, and soon he and Adam got to work on revolutionizing travel search.

They applied to Y Combinator and didn't have any trouble getting accepted, given Steve's history. Several people have asked me why Steve would do the program a second time around, giving up a chunk of equity again, despite having more experience, connections, and even personal wealth than the first time. But as I tell them—Steve is not a dumbass. He wouldn't do it if he didn't think it was worth it. So there he was going through Y Combinator again, the baby-faced graybeard in the room for those weekly dinners (you'll learn more about this in chapter 5). Another month later I found myself back on the sofa in Steve's apartment, and he had something new to show me.

Aha! Here was the invention I didn't realize I couldn't live without until I saw it. It was beautiful. All the search results in a beautiful visual layout that looked something like train schedules I remembered from European backpacking trips—and all on one page! No more scrolling through pages of results. You could easily compare flights—the duplicates were automatically hidden, along with flights no human would want to take. Oh, and just because opening multiple browser tabs was a nuisance, Steve and Adam had baked the tabs into the website. You could instantly open a new tab and compare itineraries within seconds and in one window. It was awesome, and it made sense. That's why you build. Don't tell me a story, show it to me.

We had a little less than a week to get ready for the launch, but we still had a long way to go. We didn't even have a name. Or a cute mascot. An adorable rodent was part of the plan with a name like hipmunk, since we could tell people "chipmunk without the *c*," as though that had anything to do with travel search. Admittedly, the first time I heard the name, I thought it was a cool guy with a shaved head in saffron robes. Just to be safe, we also own hipmonk.com but have no plans to expand our business into taking the agony out of tonsure.

I got to work on the branding. Fun fact: I was looking for font inspiration and grabbed the Redskins font (or at least a very similar font called Pythagoras, as in the brilliant Greek mathematician—he struck me as someone who'd have enjoyed hipmunk). It looked great in lowercase, and to this day it's the font of hipmunk.

By that time, I'd also put together the first sketches of the hipmunk himself. I was really proud of my pear-shaped chipmunk. He had buckteeth, sported a fetching aviator scarf and goggles, and pretended to fly by holding his arms outstretched, like wings in a child's imagination. I sent the first version to my girlfriend and muse, Sabriya, who said it looked like a bear with buckteeth. At least I got the buckteeth right.

Please don't go sharing this story around—I've got a reputation to uphold.

Whenever I'm working on a design, whether it's a brand or a user experience, I always rely on a small council of trusted friends to turn a fresh eye on the project and give me candid feedback. This has only gotten more valuable as I've gotten more successful, given that success seems to naturally have an inverse relationship with the amount of constructive criticism one receives. Just say no to yes-men. I'm terrified of faltering, so these people are my motivation as much as they're my inspiration.

It still needed a slight tilt—according to said muse, Sabriya—to give it that perfect touch of mirth and motion. I knew it was done when Steve's wife walked into the room, saw my monitor, and her immediate reaction was an audible "Aww!"

When I sent the final version to my dad, he told me he liked it but said, "I liked the goggles and scarf better the first time, when I saw it on Rocky the Flying Squirrel."

Right. Thanks, Dad. I vaguely remember catching reruns of that cartoon as a child. The similarity was unintentional—it came from my subconscious—but it just goes to show that we're all standing on the shoulders of giants (or giant rodents).

How to Win Deals and Influence Industry Titans

Totally unlike reddit, hipmunk has zero user-generated content; the value of the site comes from how we display the content provided by airlines and hotels. Back then, we just needed flight information (remember, minimum viable product), but we couldn't just scrape the data off airlines' websites (scraping is essentially sending software to "read" and copy content from other websites). Most important, we wanted to get paid every time someone bought a flight that we helped him or her find on hipmunk.

This was a great lesson: as the saying goes, we wanted to be "near our users' wallets." We were far from it with reddit, which made its money primarily through advertising, but we were totally there from launch day at hipmunk, thanks to some incredible hustle from Adam.

We weren't taking off unless we had airfares from providers. The data alone was invaluable because it'd make the site functional, but a business deal would also generate revenue from launch day—hipmunk would get a percentage of every ticket booked through us. Every single one of the fares on hipmunk (or on any of our competitors' sites) is the result of negotiation with a carrier or OTA (online travel agency). Those negotiations may take months, or even years, and we simply didn't have that kind of time. If we were to launch within the Y Combinator time frame (more on this in chapter 5), we had less than three months to build and launch. We needed someone to bite, because it would validate our business and help close other potential partners. Social proof in business development is not unlike fund-raising for your company (also see chapter 5). It's a dreadful catch-22 in which no one wants to do business with you unless you've already got someone doing business with you. It's similar to the challenge Steve and I had when we launched reddit with only the two of us as users while trying to encourage a community to form, which is more easily accomplished by making up fake user names than by hiring actors who pretend to be past business relationships. The way to break this particular cycle is with pure hustle, which is just what Adam did.

It started innocently enough, with phone calls and e-mails. Adam was polite and to the point, but no one responded.

When he didn't get what he wanted, Adam didn't wait for anyone's permission. He just got on a plane.

No meeting planned—he just got on a plane from SFO to ORD. He landed in Chicago and stopped by the offices of Orbitz (one of our OTA business development targets), announcing that he had some spare time to meet for a quick cup of coffee. Eventually, someone agreed, and armed with a laptop, he did a quick demo to show off what he and Steve had built. That hustle is what got us the pivotal first deal that let us launch hipmunk as planned. Then, because we had social proof, we took advantage of the same herd mentality that had previously worked against us. We may have been a tiny startup in San Francisco, but what mattered was we had a product that clients (or at least a client) wanted.

This particular deal was quite fortuitous, as Adam would discover, because we were now presenting a wide range of fare data from scores of airlines. We could approach each of these airlines with an offer to do a deal directly with them—we'd get a higher commission, and the airline would still be paying less than what they paid Orbitz. Everyone would be happy (well, maybe not Orbitz, but that's to be determined). So Adam started working his way down the list of domestic airlines, then foreign, then domestic hotels, then foreign, et cetera. Right down the list. And it all started with a plane ride and a cup of coffee.

An important coffee with Paul Graham changed our lives in chapter 2. There's another pivotal cup of joe in chapter 5. If nothing else, I hope this book convinces you to go out and drink more coffee.[2]

All Adam's debate training paid off in the boardrooms of airline and OTA executives. Once he finally got in the door—and he did some impressive things to get there, like scheduling last-minute flights and dropping notes to employees saying that he'd be in town for just a hot minute—he finally

---

2. And now you know one of the big reasons why I invested in CraftCoffee.com (a subscription artisan coffee company).

got to decision makers at some of the country's biggest airlines and OTAs.

Granted, connected investors and networking can help tremendously, but don't count on it. We have some awesome investors and advisers at hipmunk, but when it came to landing United Airlines, Adam came up empty-handed. So he went back to e-mail. Since we'd launched, we'd gotten a fabulous response from the online community and quickly became darlings of the early adopter crowd. This helped us get press, which encouraged more people to try hipmunk, which they inevitably talked about on social media, which helped us get more press, and the cycle continued. Soon Adam felt like he had enough wind at his back to try a cold e-mail to the United CEO, Jeff Smisek.

I'll dig into this more in chapter 5, but note the length and content of the e-mail Adam sent to Jeff:

> Hey. We can lower your distribution costs. Let me know who to talk to.

Adam got a response in fifteen minutes. It contained an introduction to a senior exec, and it all rolled smoothly until a deal was done and hipmunk was partnered with United Airlines, at the time the world's largest airline.[3]

The deal still took about a year to close, but its origin was that direct e-mail Adam had the audacity to send to the CEO of United Airlines. Hipmunk is a great example of the value of persistence, because travel is such a turbulent

---

3. Based on number of destinations.

industry. One has to be tenacious, because there are always layoffs, mergers, promotions, chaos. The people you build a relationship with could be at another airline or out of the industry before the ink dries.

But it worked. And knowing this is possible for the ever-changing travel industry gives me hope for almost every other industry.

On our side we had Adam Goldstein, the MIT whiz kid (damn, I must have said that to every single reporter I pitched hipmunk to) who memorized airport codes and simply would not take no for an answer; an ingenious and beautiful user interface; and an aww-inspiring mascot. But we would've been hosed without partnerships. The first one, like your first first down, is the hardest to get, but once you get it, it gives you the confidence and momentum to get more.

I can only imagine how many secretaries Adam sweet-talked. And that reminds me—bring chocolates, because winning over the people on the front lines makes a difference. Take care of the people who can take care of you. This tactic has never disappointed me; it's only pleasantly surprised me.

Sick to His Stomach on Launch Day

Of course, Steve had already launched a website once before with reddit, but that was when no one was looking. Along with all the advantages that actual experience grants us, we lose the naïveté and blind audacity that being a novice affords us. When you're a pair of nobodies launching a "social news website" in Medford, Massachusetts, no one (except maybe your mom) has high expectations for you.

You could fail a thousand times and no one would know, so why are you hesitating to launch?

Back in 2010, Steve Huffman was already well known as a top developer in the industry, and, as you know from chapter 2, reddit was (and continues to be) a great success, thanks to his work. Would his sophomore effort be a slump?

That morning, Steve told me he wanted to puke.

Fortunately, launch didn't disappoint. What a difference just five years had made. Whereas it took me months to generate any kind of attention for reddit from mainstream media, CNN reached out to *us* within twenty-four hours of hipmunk's launch. The launch was spectacular; Steve did not vomit.

I've never run an advertising campaign that cost more than a few thousand dollars. In hipmunk's case, this ended up being a billboard that greeted weary travelers on their way from SFO to the city and let them know there's an agony-free alternative to their travel search. It turns out that even the outdoor advertising industry is being disrupted by innovators like ADstruc, which brokered the deal for me. When ideas are on a level playing field, as they are on the Internet, getting your first hundred customers (or, in reddit's case, your first sixty-five million monthly users) doesn't take a huge advertising budget.

Think about it: What Super Bowl ad got you to sign up for Facebook? Social media sites win simply because people are using them and sharing their experiences on a platform (the Internet) that has every connected person in the world in the audience. Granted, there's more noise than signal, but a growing number of tools (like reddit) help us parse through it all and find the best examples of the content we're looking for (as well as content we stumble upon).

Word of mouth has always been the most powerful form of advertising, but now there are more people listening. Conversations that swayed people used to happen over watercoolers and dinner tables, but now they're being shared farther and faster than ever before on all those aforementioned social media websites. This bodes well for anyone doing something people want and communicating it well—bad news if you've got a crappy product, because instead of sending a dead-end letter to the Better Business Bureau (that was a scam, right?), now we can vent and instantly connect with other unhappy folks, and soon it snowballs into something everyone else can't help but see, too.

Because of this, launching hipmunk in 2010 was substantially easier than launching reddit in 2005, thanks largely to reddit and sites like it, which serve as platforms on which millions of people can share and find new things.

Having relationships with many members of the tech press was definitely an asset, too. These relationships are something many tech accelerators will provide for you, but having them is not required.

These days, there are so many more of us connected and sharing that it's nearly impossible for something with any degree of novelty or usefulness to go unnoticed. I'll break it all down in chapter 5, but the media are everywhere. Incidentally, reddit is a big part of that and was quite a boon for launching hipmunk ('twas all part of the very, very long-term plan!).

I asked one of the inbound press requesters how she had

heard about us—Hacker News (News.YCombinator.com—a reddit for startup news). Journalists are getting story ideas from us. And why not? The zeitgeist has never been more evident, so it makes sense to write about what we're already starting to buzz about.

This successful launch story is rather typical. Build something people want, launch it to the world, try not to vomit, and see what happens.

A few months after our launch, Kayak, a major competitor, filed their S-1.[4] And it didn't matter. It didn't matter that one of our many competitors had already made $128 million in revenue that year and was looking to raise another $50 million. We didn't need to ask anyone's permission, certainly not theirs, to start a competitor. We'd simply built a better travel search experience and we believed we could win with superior execution.

Kayak inadvertently did us a favor just months after we'd launched. At a major travel summit, the Kayak CEO was asked about hipmunk, and he declared, "I find their bravado refreshing. I find their product unremarkable. [...] The Internet's a busy highway. I hope they don't end up as roadkill." He couldn't have done us a bigger favor, and Adam shrewdly capitalized on it when he took the stage. He announced, "I'm Adam Goldstein, CEO of hipmunk, the startup that Kayak's CEO can't stop talking about."

Online, an upstart company of three people in a San Francisco apartment is immediately on the same playing

---

4. http://techcrunch.com/2010/11/17/travel-search-engine-kayak-files-for-50 -million-ipo/

field with a multi-million-dollar company preparing to go public. And we can win. All our investors are betting on it.

Revolutionaries in Cairo

"And that's how we know we're on to something with hipmunk. Questions?"

I made sure to put extra cat photos in my slide presentation for the forty or so Egyptian entrepreneurs in the audience. I figured it couldn't hurt.

I was there at the Marriott in Cairo just a few weeks after the social media–fueled revolution that toppled Hosni Mubarak's regime. In fact, I was speaking as part of a collaboration between the US and Danish governments designed to win hearts and minds by providing mentorship for Egyptian Internet entrepreneurs. Just weeks earlier, Mubarak had literally turned off the Internet in Egypt. Now here I was answering questions—the same questions I get asked by startup founders in Brooklyn—for a group of Egyptian revolutionaries. Not the bullshit kind of "revolutionaries" people like me are sometimes called for the work we've done to build companies or nonprofits—these men and women had brought down an authoritarian government and were now working to rebuild their country through entrepreneurship on the open Internet.

Talk about inspirational. I didn't leave the Marriott until long after nightfall. We were speaking and mentoring during daylight hours, and the entire group buzzed over dinner with stories and perspectives from the Egyptian founders, whom we'd had the privilege to meet. It was a mix of young and old, American and European, but we were all united in awe of the founders, who were hungry to bring their dreams to fruition online. I barely saw the Great Pyramid, but frankly, I didn't mind. Inside the obligatory photo of me in front of one of the Seven Wonders of the Ancient World, rocking a hipmunk shirt I designed, of course, is a person beaming because he had a hunch validated.

This was the first time in all my travels that I'd seen a situation like this. Living and volunteering in my own homeland, Armenia, for three months exposed me firsthand to the relentless resourcefulness of entrepreneurs at all levels of society. But even with all Armenia's woes, the country was nothing close to the rough state Egypt was in when I met with my startup peers there. They faced far, far more challenges than I did in the process of getting their companies going. And they were doing it with the same bullish ambitions in spite of tremendous hardships, such as a thirty-year dictatorship that had been recently overthrown by a haphazard collective of revolutionaries with the hope of crowdsourcing a constitution and holding Egypt's first free and fair election in decades. They had no hesitation. They were as fearless as any other entrepreneurs you'd meet, only they had legitimate fears in a country that was figuratively and literally rebuilding.

Taking the agony out of travel also turns out to be the basis for a viable business in many contexts, including on the congested streets of Cairo. That's what five cousins—Aly Rafea, Mohamed Rafea, Gamal Sadek, Mostafa Beltagy, and Yehia Ismail—are doing with Bey2ollak (it's Egyptian slang, used when telling someone about something you've heard), a mobile application (iOS, Android, BlackBerry, Windows, and even Nokia!) that allows commuters to crowdsource more effective routes to avoid the city's notoriously awful traffic. Turn on the app and check road conditions updated by your fellow drivers. Return the favor next time you're stuck in traffic with a simple touch (select red for bad, yellow for meh, and green for clear). It works. And it doesn't require expensive infrastructure or—you guessed it—anyone's permission.

The app launched supporting only one platform, BlackBerry, and ended the day with five thousand installs. When I met them in Cairo, they had expanded to multiple mobile platforms and had tens of thousands of users. Today, Bey2ollak has hundreds of thousands of active users. And they started it all without spending a single Egyptian pound on advertising. The same online platforms that let Egyptians coordinate protests and share their revolution with the world also let them share their secret for beating traffic. The same social media strategies that I've been using for a travel startup based in San Francisco are working for a traffic-fighting startup based in Cairo. And why not?

Building an audience doesn't require a large advertising budget, certainly not at the beginning. Making something people want—something that people love, that solves a real problem they have in an elegant way—is the most effective thing one can do to generate buzz. There's no secret to "going viral," despite what plenty of self-appointed "social media gurus" may tell you (hint: if they call themselves that, run in the opposite direction). What online success stories have in common isn't a cute mascot (but seriously, at least consider it); it's tenacity. As my EgyptAir flight took off, I regretted not booking it on hipmunk, but more important, I realized there really is something special going on online in Egypt.

I'm playing a small part in this massive network, but in Cairo and throughout the world, there are great ideas and talented people to pull them off—people who have an opportunity they simply did not have even a decade ago. And it's unlike anything we can even fathom.

Holy shit. This "Internet" thing is gonna be big.

A Year In, I'm Out

After a little more than a year of running the marketing and community building for hipmunk, essentially from my apartment in New York, I moved into an advisory role while we searched for someone to take over who'd be based in San Francisco.

I didn't realize it then, but the timing couldn't have been better. Without a full-time job on my mind, I turned my attention to my social enterprise, Breadpig, and signed the deal to write this book. Then a few weeks later, I learned that two bills, SOPA and PIPA, were before the House and Senate respectively and were poised to pass before year's end. If they passed, they would do considerable damage to Internet innovation, not to mention free speech. With the extra time on my hands, I dove into the fight and found myself meeting legislators in Washington a week later. I was subsequently invited to testify in front of the House, and I appeared in *The New York Times* as one of the faces of the opposition movement.

In the year that followed my exit from hipmunk, *Forbes* magazine called me mayor of the Internet,[5] and then, after we concluded our Internet 2012 Bus Tour across the heartland of America, BuzzFeed went all-in, saying I was running for president of the Internet.[6] I was also included on *Forbes*'s 30 under 30 list, twice. Now, with my thirtieth birthday on the horizon, I look at twenty-two-year-olds with a bit of envy, but mostly awe. They're much further along at that age than Steve and I were. I've got more work to do, but it's going to be fun watching and helping where I can as hipmunk continues to soar.

Not only is hipmunk growing as a business, it's also growing as a company. At the time of this writing, it has just closed its Series B financing and employs thirty people in a new office in San Francisco. I continue spreading the word about hipmunk's little rodent and handing out luggage tags to excited fans. Hipmunk is on a great course, and I'm extremely proud of everything it's done so far and will undoubtedly continue to do. We have no idea what's in store for ourselves or our businesses. That's life, accelerated, on the Internet.

In good times and bad, *be relentlessly resourceful.* And always be giving damns, lots of damns, about what you do, whether it's the things you make or the service you provide.

---

5. http://www.forbes.com/sites/andygreenberg/2012/06/05/how-reddits-alexis-ohanian-became-the-mayor-of-the-internet/

6. http://www.buzzfeed.com/jwherrman/why-is-this-man-running-for-president-of-the-inter

PART II

CHAPTER FOUR

Startup MBA Part I—Make Something People Love

I've got this great idea....

Everyone

Here's the thing about ideas: ideas are worthless. That might sound harsh, but my experience has been that execution is everything.

You might be thinking, "But what if someone steals my idea?" Trust me: most of us don't have the spare time to start a company with your great idea, and even if we did, it's going to be up to you to outexecute your competitors. You're going to be dealing with competition from the day you launch, so you better learn to stop caring about them right now.

Far too often, founders are so enamored of perfecting their ideas that they don't even want to tell people about them. And then when they launch, they're suddenly put in the position of having to tell their idea to everyone who'll listen.

Even better than telling is showing. In fact, any discussions you have—with advisers, potential investors, or clients—aren't terribly valuable before you have a prototype. You need something to actually talk about—and test. The job of a good investor or adviser is to digest this and to ask tough questions. It's not to embarrass you, it's to see how you think and then help you diagnose the current state of your business and get you to the next step.

Since co-founding reddit with Steve and starting more companies after it, I've invested in more than sixty tech startups and advised hundreds more through my role at Y Combinator. It's given me a valuable perspective on many different startup scenarios that all serve as real-world lessons—some of these companies have been acquired, others have imploded, some continue to soar, and others are still finding their way.

The one thing they all have in common is that they've "pivoted" at some point. At least, that's the popular euphemism for "failed and adapted" these days. But no matter what it's called, early-stage companies are bound to change their ideas along the way. It could be dramatic—like an entirely different market or a brand-new product—or it could be more subtle. But either way, a company that's just a few months old is going to be different a year later. At this early stage, we invest largely in people, because, as I said, ideas are cheap. Another reason not to get married to your ideas, even the ones that seem perfect.

Steve's pre-reddit idea, My Mobile Menu (but really, who could forget MMM!?), came about because Steve hated waiting in line for his take-out food even though he already knew what he wanted before he walked into the restaurant. Steve thought he'd found a solution to one of modern life's most vexing problems, but most people didn't agree.[1] So we had to find another problem to solve. What we settled on was our desire to know what was going on in the world at all times, and our frustration at the lack of a single, always fresh front page for the Internet. Then, as you know by now, we found our audience.

Our friends from the Y Combinator summer class of 2005, Justin Kan and Emmett Shear, sold their company, Kiko.com, for $258,100 (on eBay, of all places) when Google launched their web-based calendar. The Google calendar's integration was so tight with Gmail that the writing was on the wall for Kiko. The Kiko team, ever the intrepid founders, used the sale as an opportunity to pivot. They repaid their investors and dove into Justin.tv, which is now the world's leading live streaming video company. In the early stages, surrounding yourself with the right people is infinitely more important than having a good idea. Your relationship with your co-founder(s) is what's more likely to make or break your company than your idea itself.[2] Picking a co-founder is actually quite a bit like marriage, only there's no sex—though from what I've learned from married couples, that's actually just like marriage.

---

1. Turns out Steve was just ahead of his time. Now, thanks to the near ubiquity of smartphones, there are quite a few apps that address the problem My Mobile Menu was intended to solve. One I've invested in is called OrderAhead, which will, I hope, validate Steve's idea, albeit a decade later.

2. Do not actually marry your co-founder. You can, of course, but it's not required.

Identify Genuine Need

The Internet, unlike your mom, is fickle and ruthless (unless your mom is also fickle and ruthless, in which case you should have a leg up on your competitors). Attention spans are short, and there's always a cute cat video just a click away. That means you've got to be compelling. And you've absolutely got to make something people actually want or they'll never stick around, let alone come back.

I encounter plenty of startup founders who have a great technology they've engineered and shoehorn that into a solution that they hope people will want. To me, this route is much harder than identifying a real problem first and then solving it as simply as possible.

Worse are the founders who aren't able to build anything yet and are simply brainstorming and drawing mock-ups in the vacuum of their own heads. Find your customers right now and talk to them. Are they just being polite? Bear in mind that most people don't like giving bad (honest) feedback. That positive reinforcement about your idea doesn't mean a thing until someone actually pays you or until you see repeat, engaged visitors coming to your website.

So how do you make something that people actually want? Start with a real problem.

Obviously it should be a problem for you, but be sure it's also a problem for others. The thing is, sometimes people don't realize they have a problem. And often just telling them they have a problem will only elicit an "Oh, that's good enough for me." As the old cliché goes, we're creatures of habit. It's really hard to persuade someone to try your thing when the status quo is good enough. But put a better solution in front of the same person and suddenly the status quo looks repugnant.

This is precisely what happened with hipmunk. Few people Adam or Steve spoke with before launch thought there was a problem with how they searched for flights. They took for granted that you had to sift through tons of terrible flights and hunt across a mess of tabs for the best itinerary. It wasn't until we launched and consumers saw our agony-free alternative that they realized how bad everything else was by comparison.

You've undoubtedly encountered products or services that have frustrated you. Keep a notepad handy—I prefer digital, but analog is fine, too—and write down whatever is upsetting you. There's a good chance you'll find a business in those notes.

Remember, Adam's awful experiences booking flights for the MIT debate team motivated him to start hipmunk because he figured there had to be a better way to search for flights online. Similarly, Airbnb got its start because the founders needed to pay their rent and realized there were lots of other people who would pay to rent the founders' unused space.

So many successful companies start out like this: the founders were having a problem, and they found a way to solve it. A company doesn't have to start this way, but it's the easiest place to start. Make something you'd use (and, ideally, pay money for). That's what we did in the case of reddit and hipmunk (the latter being the one having a baked-in business model from day zero).

Another starting point is to have an idea that very few people other than the founders can actually *build*. These technical feats provide a natural defense against competition: remember, every hard problem you solve drops a massive obstacle in front of anyone who'd want to replicate you. Certain problems haven't been solved because none of the few people smart enough to do so have made it happen. Look at something like Google, which Larry and Sergey were technically capable of building at a time when not many people were. Back then, there were very few people smart enough to build their own search engine, let alone imbue it with software that could crawl and rank the entire World Wide Web.

There's also a third route: think of an idea that is rooted in a perspective that everyone else is missing because they don't see the potential *today*. A friend and fellow startup dude, Chris Dixon, describes the extreme version of this by saying, "The next big thing will start out looking like a toy."[3] One example of this would be Kickstarter. Their first project, Drawing for Dollars, surpassed its humble twenty-dollar goal by raising thirty-five dollars, which came from three backers who bought artwork from an artist in Long Island City.[4] Less than three years later, a team using the same platform raised ten million dollars in preorders for a futuristic watch called Pebble.[5] The idea of a group of people pitching in to make something come to fruition is

---

3. http://cdixon.org/2010/01/03/the-next-big-thing-will-start-out-looking-like -a-toy/

4. http://www.kickstarter.com/projects/darkpony/drawing-for-dollars

5. http://www.kickstarter.com/projects/597507018/pebble-e-paper-watch-for -iphone-and-android

hardly novel, but the way the Kickstarter team leveraged the Internet to pitch to millions of people simultaneously (as opposed to a coterie of traditional investors) certainly was.

Know What You're Doing

Once you've identified a problem, you might be tempted to dive right in and start trying to solve it. But you need to do your homework first. That means research.

One of my portfolio companies, ELaCarte, which builds software to enable restaurant customers to order and pay through a tablet, was founded by a talented MIT grad, Raj Suri, who really wanted to understand the business he was diving into. When he first pitched me, he explained with the measured words of an engineer that he'd gotten a job as a waiter. An MIT PhD—a waiter? My former-Pizza-Hut-waiter heart grew three sizes that day.

I can't tell you how many people in his position would've started building something before actually figuring out what his market wanted. Sure, it's easier to solve a problem without talking to your potential users, but odds are you're going to be building something for a bigger market than just yourself and your peer group. Raj got out from behind the keyboard to really understand the industry he was targeting before he disrupted it.

RentHop, a Y Combinator startup that was poised to be the hipmunk of apartment rentals, just needed some more love. Its two technically brilliant founders had devised some very clever ways to sift through and find the gems among the mountains of notoriously awful apartment rental listings in New York City. But the company began when one of the founders, Lee Lin, got so frustrated by his own renting experience that he got his broker's license in order to really understand what it was like on both sides.

If you're not willing to really understand the industry you're aspiring to reinvent, don't bother starting a startup. Having industry experience is not only invaluable for building a great product or service, it also shows investors the dedication a successful founder needs to have.

Business First, Then Business Cards

Once you've identified a real problem and done your research, start trying to solve it in the simplest way possible. Your first version should certainly embarrass you. "Minimum viable product" has become a startup cliché for good reason. Just build the simplest possible solution to a problem, and launch it.

This probably won't take as long as you might think. Each round of Y Combinator was designed to be three months long because Paul wanted it to be a summer program, so students could decide to take time off from school if their company was going well. This happened to also be a reasonable amount of time to go from idea to a live product. If it takes longer than a few months to start testing your idea, it's because either you're trying too hard to perfect it (you *never* will, so don't bother) or there's some other bigger problem.

The first version of reddit was absurdly simple. We didn't have voting, and we certainly didn't have commenting or the ability to create subreddits. It was simply a place where one could submit links and, based on clicks, see them rise and fall on the front page. A new user would simply see a front page of interesting links to click on.

Hipmunk was a flight-only search when we launched (no hotels, car rentals, etc.), and even that was strikingly bare-bones. Thanks to Adam's hustle with the online travel agencies, we not only provided flight data but also started to collect a commission on referrals right away. We were making money from day one, which always puts a smile on investors' faces.

And bear this in mind: the first version of Airbnb, the startup that has more rooms available for rent than the Hilton corporation, started from a single apartment in the SOMA neighborhood of San Francisco. The founders began the site by renting out air mattresses in their own home to conference attendees looking to save money.

Once you're up and running, spread the word and start watching how users interact with what you've built. Listen to how they're talking about it. This is key. There's something incredibly satisfying about seeing the logs of the first users who try out what you've built. It's one reason why I can't encourage enough students to start building projects just for the experience of having real people all over the world use something you've built. Compared to dull school-work, learning by creating something relevant and usable is incredibly rewarding.

Once you've got something to show, use the growing number of available tools that allow people to share that great idea. We launched reddit in 2005, before "social media" was a phrase. Just five years later, launching hipmunk was drastically easier, because by then there were more tools than ever for people to spread the word about things they care about.

Word of mouth has always been the most powerful form of advertising—and it spreads faster and farther than ever before. Make something people want, and people will find out about it. If you're not getting traction, it simply means you haven't solved that core problem of making something people want. But that's okay! Figure out what people *are* using. Talk to your users—those first hundred or so people who are willing to take a chance on a product they've never heard of are golden. Treat them well and get to the root of whatever problem it is that you're not currently solving for them.

The most striking example of this was the stagnant first year of Airbnb.com. What it took was for the founders to actually stay in the homes of their dogged users to find out what kept them using the site and how they could improve their experience.

Perhaps the most distilled version of this would be to simply give a damn about everything you're building. Take pride in the products you make, the service you provide, and the company you build. Give more damns than anyone else, because there aren't a lot of things a startup has going for it, except that its founders and employees certainly care more than the competition. And that makes all the difference.

Why Are You Still Reading This Book?

One of the great equalizing effects of the World Wide Web is the fact that the cost of starting a company online falls every day. Your address is a URL. If someone has a browser anywhere in the world without a firewall (i.e., not in China), your idea is as easily accessible to that person as anything else online. You may have the best blueberry muffin recipe in town, but if your bakery isn't on the right street, it could be game over. Location, location, location, right?

Remember—online, all links (locations) are created equal. And it costs about ten dollars to register a domain for a year.

The biggest investment you'll need to make is your time. If you're already a web developer, pretend this is a "choose your own adventure" and head to page 103, because you're already ahead of the game.

Find People Who Give a Damn

All right, now that the developers are gone...

Here's the thing. On the Internet, the makers wield all the power. Remember, if they needn't ask for anyone's permission, creatives can just create. If you're looking to build a website and you're not a builder, you're more than likely going to have to try to become one. Now, you might be thinking, "Wait—I can just hire one, right?" Of course you can try, but demand far outweighs supply when it comes to developers in the developed world, and this isn't likely to change very soon. I'm encouraging all the geeks I know to reproduce for the sake of humanity, but it'll still be years before their sons and daughters will be of programming age.

What about outsourcing? I've never done it, because if something goes wrong (and it will), whether it's 3:00 a.m. or 3:00 p.m. Eastern time, I need to know that my CTO is either awake or willing to wake up and give a damn about solving the problem. Unless you've got a close relationship with whoever is overseas and is working with you, it's going to be nearly impossible to expect the same kind of dedication from that person.

That said, I've seen startups successfully build a minimum viable product that can get some users, show some traction, and ultimately be rebuilt from scratch by whoever takes over as CTO. I've also seen startups entirely outsource development and, by building a strong team behind a reliable point person, actually maintain it over the years of scale and growth.

Frankly, the most valuable thing you can do as you build something online is learn how to write code. Even if you end up never starting something of your own, the skills you learn in development are highly sought after these days. Plus it doesn't show any signs of slowing down, given that in the future, everything that turns on will also have software.

Good news! All the greatest developers (like Steve said in chapter 2) are predominantly self-taught, thanks to a wealth of resources available online—for free!

That's right. You can learn one of the most marketable skills right now from your home for the cost of a computer, an Internet connection, and your time.

The options vary greatly, but here are four suggestions to get you started—three I invested in because of how much I believe in the value of this education and one with zombies:

http://Codecademy.com
http://GeneralAssemb.ly
http://MakeGamesWithUs.com
http://RailsForZombies.org (I didn't invest in this one, but it's awesome.)

Once you understand how a website is created and have gone through the process of designing a user experience, you'll never look at websites the same way. This goes for everything from the choice of fonts to the layout of buttons to the copy on the screen. Keep an eye out for great design that inspires you and keep that list beside the list of agonizing experiences I encouraged you to write. You'll start seeing every bad experience online as an opportunity for innovation.

Thanks largely to the success of Y Combinator, tech accelerators became a common model for, you guessed it, *accelerating* startup innovation. Not all accelerators are created equal, and even getting into Y Combinator is no guarantee of success. Fortunately, as the cost of starting something online continues to fall, the opportunities for getting it funded continue to grow.

Earn Every Single User

This isn't just important for your product, it's important for everything you produce—every e-mail, all the copy on your website, even your business card. You'll need to get everyone (other than your mom) to care about what you're working on. To this day, I remind myself of this every time I create something, including this book. If I'm not entertaining, informing, or inspiring you—what's the point? I need to earn your attention.

Now you know why there are doodles in this book.

How to Surprise and Delight

I teased you about this earlier. There's no point in trying to found a startup until you've got something people want. Once you've got traction, it's time to focus on turning those users/customers/donors into evangelists by doing a full-scale analysis of all the ways you can build a company and community that not only understands why you're doing what you do but will also be your best advertising for it.

This started as a class I taught at one of the New York locations of General Assembly, an education startup teaching skills for tech entrepreneurship, but after a half-dozen sold-out classes I realized I needed a way for it to scale. That's where this section comes in!

Whether you're building your brand around communities, as reddit does; around design, as hipmunk does; or around connection, as Breadpig does, one thing is clear: how much you care really does matter. Many of us interact with the Internet through beautifully designed hardware that is ultimately still robotic, no matter how shiny. A chance to surprise and delight someone by doing something a little exceptional goes a long way because it provides a smack of awesome humanity upside the head. There is nothing insignificant. That error message you just wrote is probably just like thousands of others I've encountered and will encounter—make it different; make it sound like your brand. For example, when I make a mistake on hipmunk and put in an arrival date that's actually before my departure date, the error message is anything but generic:

We don't support trips to the past yet.

Think of how much that conveys in just thirty-two characters. Instead of Error: Invalid dates, you get a cheeky reply that probably makes you smile a bit.

That's something Steve dropped in because he felt like it and didn't need to file a report to get it done. And it makes a difference. I routinely see people chortling about this online. And that's just one example of many—not unique to hipmunk but unique to a new generation of companies building products and services that actually give a damn about the end customer.

How bad has it gotten?

My friend and fellow author Tony Hsieh, who's also published by Business Plus, wrote a major international bestseller, *Delivering Happiness*, that essentially boiled down to two points: excellent customer service is vital to Zappos, and it should be vital in your business, too. Think about that. What does it say about the state of business when CEOs everywhere hear that and think, "Wow! That's a revolutionary idea—we should be treating our customers well!"

There's a huge opportunity here for startups. It's one more reason why the best time is now to get started—so many incumbents are still figuring this out. Most of them will never get the Internet because they weren't raised online. Use that knowledge to your advantage, founder.

In the meantime, I'll also inevitably be consulting for some of these companies, telling them to adapt or die. We'll see who gets the message, but there really is hope for everyone.

One of the most reviled organizations in the United States—the Internal Revenue Service[6]—inadvertently demonstrated that. In 2010, a San Francisco couple scanned a letter they received from the IRS and put it online. There's a portion of the letter that I love to share. Here's the best part:

> We have reviewed your correspondence regarding the penalties that were charged to your account and based on your explanation that "the adult brain turns to jello those first few months raising a baby," we have decided to remove all penalty charges. A total of $2,522.00 in penalty charges have been removed.

Yep, that happened. Not only did a kind soul at the IRS have the creativity and autonomy to do that, but he or she couldn't have expected the impact it made in our connected world. Ten years ago this story would've made the rounds at the couple's workplaces and probably at the next family Thanksgiving. Maybe it would have reached a few dozen or maybe a hundred people.

How did I find it? It was voted to the top of a popular subreddit, where it soared across Twitter, Facebook, et cetera. (It even was quoted in those awkward e-mails your parents still forward around.) Millions of people online saw this letter and were affected by it. Some person in the bureaucratic, form-letter jungle of the IRS had enough imagination, initiative, and humanity to make a $2,522 decision that did

---

6. And just to be clear, auditors, I love paying my taxes.

more for the reputation of the IRS than a multi-million-dollar ad campaign ever could have.

Just think of the potential Super Bowl commercial: "The IRS loves you—honest! See you April 15!"

There aren't enough talking geckos and Old Spice guys in the world to genuinely convince anyone that the IRS gives a damn about the individual. But letters like this one actually might win a few people over. And if the IRS can do it, why can't you?

Ignore Thy Competition

This was something Steve and I learned just a few weeks after launching reddit. (If only I'd had this book to read before we launched![7]) On July 11, 2005, I sent an e-mail to Steve under the subject line READ THIS that contained only three words and a URL:

www.digg.com
meet the enemy.

The next day, I signed up for Digg to learn just what we were dealing with. Steve and I hadn't done a very thorough competitive analysis before we got started speccing reddit, but it turned out to be a blessing because we didn't have anything else clouding our judgment during those weeks we

---

7. To anyone reading this with access to a time machine: first, congrats! Second, after you're done killing Hitler, would you mind handing the twenty-two-year-old me this book? Also, you might as well include a sports almanac from your time, too. Thanks!

built the site. What doomed so many startups in our space was that they essentially copied Digg—and every one of them, like Digg, eventually fell. Back then, though, we didn't know how it would turn out. I just knew I'd be answering "How are you different from Digg?" questions for the foreseeable future. Fortunately, we'd built a fundamentally different platform, even if it took us longer to gain traction.

Digg launched in December of 2004, when their founder, Kevin Rose, promoted it on the TV show he co-hosted, *The Screen Savers*[8] (he didn't mention it was *his* website, but so it goes). All of a sudden we had competition. And it was started by a quasi-celebrity who'd already used his platform to jump-start the community and who'd already raised a round of funding.

Meanwhile, two nobodies fresh out of college had just taken twelve grand to pay for spaghetti and were working on solving a similar problem. I loved those odds.

Naturally, we mentioned Digg to our lead investor, Paul Graham, who gave us some sage advice that's remained indispensable to this day: Digg wasn't going to defeat us. We'd either defeat ourselves first or they would defeat themselves for us.

If you're solving an interesting problem, or just having success, there will always be competition. Online, the marketplace of ideas is so fluid that new entrants can have tremendous success in a short period of time (and existing players can fall off just as fast). One ought to be more concerned about an upstart drinking one's milk shake than

---

8. http://www.youtube.com/watch?v=W1_YoG7lqI4

about an incumbent, but in either case, it doesn't behoove you to be looking back at competitors because you'll find yourself lulled into replicating and reacting instead of innovating and moving forward.

As we kept improving reddit, Digg kept making missteps. The value of both our websites is that the community created and curated all the great content. Steve and I recognized this, and thus every technological and business decision Steve and I made had this central truth in mind—Digg, not so much.

That said, it took awhile for everyone else to realize it. As early as 2008, Erick Schonfeld, writer for a popular tech blog at the time, *TechCrunch*, had already written us off, saying, "The winner here clearly is Digg," and calling the gap between us "pretty insurmountable."[9] There was a moment, still years before reddit's traffic passed and then eclipsed Digg's, that I'll never forget (well, that and it's on YouTube). In 2009, while Kevin Rose was onstage for a live event, someone threw a homemade reddit shirt at his feet. He picked it up and showed it to the crowd. Then he pantomimed blowing his nose on the shirt and discarded it.[10] This was too good.

Just a year after blowing his nose on reddit, reddit blew Digg out of the way. All we had to do was ignore it—Digg's own missteps caught up with it and the site's popularity plummeted. To this day, reddit continues to soar, but no

9. http://techcrunch.com/2008/06/18/reddit-tries-to-compete-the-open -source-way/

10. http://www.youtube.com/watch?v=xyqe7A5ombA

one is complacent. Our competition is now much bigger and broader as we battle for everyone's attention online. The advantage of leading is that you're not following anyone, but as I said, the competition to worry about is what is probably launching right now.[11]

Love Thy Haters

Long before the glorious day of our acquisition, we were just grateful that Y Combinator had let us into their exclusive program after a dramatic rejection. This program, with Paul at the helm, was oriented toward key developers, who really do have all the leverage in this industry. I was one of only two "nontechnical founders" in the program. Despite having programming experience in high school and college, I was devoting my time to doing "everything else" at the company, though that assertion was met with quite a bit of skepticism. A running joke that Steve had to endure at Y Combinator meetings was "What does Alexis do?" One of the advisers in the program even overheard me speaking German (I'm proficient, thanks to my mother) and remarked to Steve, "Alexis sounds much more intelligent in German."

I didn't think I sounded that dumb in English. Fortunately, as a guy who grew up with the name Alexis, I quickly learned that it's those with the lowest self-confidence who belittle and bully other people. When it comes to put-downs,

---

11. Speaking of which, if you are reading this book and starting the company that will trump reddit, please let me know so I can at least find some solace in knowing that my book helped another founder.

I ran out of "fucks" to give back in grade school, so now I just embrace it.

When we launched reddit, I made a note of the exceptionally bad feedback we got. There weren't a lot of haters, but the bad feedback was incredibly useful. I printed out all our most vitriolic and negative feedback and created a "wall of negative reinforcement" beside my desk. I quoted people who said that we weren't doing anything innovative and weren't going to have a chance—a particularly clever commenter renamed the Summer Founders Program the Summer Flounders Program. We were the first Y Combinator startup to launch, after all, so although not many people had heard of the project run by Paul Graham and his associates, the ones who did trained their gaze directly on us. I loved all the negative feedback. The more baseless, the better. I wanted to know exactly whom I'd be working to prove wrong.

My favorite piece of motivation would come a few months after we launched. We hustled a meeting with Google, thanks to a fortunate (albeit slightly strategic) seat I took beside Chris Sacca, Google's head of special initiatives, at a dinner that Paul had organized after our first startup school. We hit it off well enough, and Chris sounded open to having Steve and me visit Mountain View the next time we were in town. Score. Once we had a meeting with Google, it seemed prudent to also try to schedule something with Yahoo!, too (I'm not sure what their share price will look like when you're reading this book, but back in 2005 they were actively acquiring young teams that embraced popular technology, such as del.icio.us and Flickr).

Our Google meeting went splendidly. We met with scores of people and even ended up getting an acquisition offer that Steve and I turned down. There's no better confidence boost than turning down an acquisition offer, especially from a nerd-tastic company like Google, but it's also terrifying, because you don't want to regret it.

Yahoo! was a different story. After a cheery meeting in Mountain View, we went down to Sunnyvale for a chat with some Yahoo! folks. In short, they were not impressed.

We took them through a demo and talked about our traffic numbers, which admittedly weren't all that impressive back then. Our company was still only a few months old, and Steve and I were still a two-person company, but we hoped they'd see the same promise in us that Google had.

Out of nowhere, the guy who was running the meeting said:

"You are a rounding error compared to Yahoo!"[12]

He said it flatly, smothered in a hearty condescension sauce. Maybe it was just part of a very strange negotiation strategy, but after that the meeting went quickly downhill. We left soon thereafter, fired up our Metallica mix CD (yes, I know), and took our rental car back to SFO. Back in Boston, I printed out a new piece of paper that would become the centerpiece of my wall. It had only five words on it:

YOU ARE A ROUNDING ERROR.

Those five words still motivate me to this day. And that

---

12. He didn't yell it, but whenever one writes Yahoo!, one is obliged to include an exclamation point.

executive is still working in the ranks of Silicon Valley, still (I hope) fueling the fire inside more founders like me.

You Can't Make Progress When You're Not Taking Steps

It's not all "up and to the right" (the direction of the line on a traffic chart that tracks soaring logarithmic growth) for startups. Most of them will never enjoy that kind of growth. Reddit certainly never did. Instead, you'll have weeks when user growth (or customer growth, or another kind of growth) isn't moving up as fast as you'd like, or not moving at all, or worse, going down. The latter is the best time to spur your team to action, but the other situations are seductive, since plenty of founders are lulled into an "It'll get better" mentality. It can, but only if you start attacking the problems.

What's a good place to start? Customers. Users. The people you're trying to prevail upon to care about your business.

Outliers are outliers, remember, so instead of being disappointed when you're not the next Facebook, be happy to be your own company that solves a real problem with an elegant solution and wins in a market that's underserved. Investors want to know they're going to get a return on their money despite the terrible odds, and investors realize that Mark Zuckerbergs aren't born every day (thankfully, given the identity crisis Mark would have—though there is at least one child named Facebook in Egypt).[13]

---

13. http://articles.cnn.com/2011-02-21/world/egypt.child.facebook_1_facebook -page-wael-ghonim-social-media?_s=PM:WORLD

Experience is traditionally undervalued in the tech sector because we're accustomed to the wunderkind myth. But that being said, there are so many things I'd end up being smarter about if I had reddit to do all over again. Fortunately, Steve and I applied these lessons to hipmunk. For instance, back then I remember worrying a lot about designing business cards. In fact, I've still got my original business cards from reddit, and they terrify me. I was learning my way through Photoshop, and it shows. I also have no idea why Steve and I both chose the title Director.

Phone number censored for the sake of whoever has it now.

Focusing too much on a rather inconsequential item, such as business cards, underscores a larger problem I had with relinquishing control to more talented people—also known as delegation—which becomes even more important as the team grows.

Find People Who Give a Damn;
Hire Them; Repeat

A startup will begin its life in your head. Maybe you'll start building it yourself, or maybe you'll recruit some friends to help you. Those first team members, whether they join as founders or employees, have a tremendous impact on your company's fate.

You cannot succeed with a broken team, so hire wisely and fire quickly. One ideal quality in an employee can be best summed up as: "Gives a damn." I've heard it called different things by my peers, but you should be hiring people who take pride in their work. Whether they're developers or salespeople, if they don't give a damn about the mission of the company and the quality of their work, you and your team will suffer.

Startups have so little going for them. They start out unknown, understaffed, and underfunded. That means decisions like early hires become priorities of the greatest magnitude. You see, the primary advantage you have is your absolute focus on solving a specific problem better than anyone else. Larger companies simply cannot have that kind of focused dedication, nor can they inspire a work ethic as passionately as a startup can (another reason why it's not worth paying attention to the competition, because it's the ones you don't know about yet that are probably going to be drinking your milk shake).

To get you started, here's a list of questions I like to ask potential hires:

- ☐ What have you built? What interests me most is what you've built outside of work.
- ☐ You're interviewing for job X, but how do you feel about doing Y, which is only barely within the scope of X?
- ☐ What about working at a startup appeals to you?
- ☐ You've got a week left to live—we can safely assume I've given you the week off. What do you do?
- ☐ What's the last awesome thing you learned?
- ☐ If you could do literally anything you wanted for a living, what would it be?
- ☐ What's your spirit animal?

There's no perfect checklist for interviews, but the question I ask every time is the first one on the list: What have you built? I would rather see evidence that a person has built something of quality than evidence of a perfect GPA. In startups, GTD (Getting Things Done) matters more than GPA. At an early-stage company, where you went to school matters less than what you have actually done, because we're all going to have a variety of responsibilities, many of which we'll be learning how to handle as we go along. In fact, many of the characteristics of a great early hire are the same as those of a founder. If you've demonstrated the ability to create things and take pride in your work, then I need to know you're a good culture fit. What are you passionate about? *Star Wars* or *Star Trek*? I've made hiring decisions without knowing a person's major because I knew what she had done and what she could do on the team.[14]

---

14. And because she preferred *Star Wars*.

Awesome people feed off one another and combine to form something greater than the individual parts—like Voltron.

If you've had the pleasure of working with an elite team, you know what a difference it makes. And if you haven't, you know what it's like when it's not working. And it's bad.

So what sorts of people do you actually want on your team? In early versions of Y Combinator, Paul Graham used to ask teams to tell him something about each founder that shows how that person is an "animal." Here's how we responded in our application:[15]

Animals? We're a freaking zoo....[16]

Steve regularly works extra hours at his current programming job, even when overtime isn't an option (i.e., working for free), to fix nagging bugs. At school, Steve often works late nights with computer science friends helping them get assignments working....

When it comes to design, Alexis literally won't rest until every pixel is aligned—sleep deprivation is the status quo, and when it comes to working in general, coffee makes sure he's the last one to go to sleep at night and the first one up in the morning.

The difference between working with people who care and working with those who don't is vast, and the repercussions don't just lie in the work they do but in every element of your interactions with them. Surely you've been in jobs

15. http://alexisohanian.com/our-y-combinator-summer-05-application-what-w
16. Steve's joke.

with co-workers who just don't care, let alone take pride in their work. It's a nuisance in those situations, but when it's your own company, it's absolute poison.

From the Investor's Perspective

Having had hundreds (thousands?) of cups of coffee with startup founders, I've become aware of some interesting trends, and although I'm by no means a perfect investor, I've identified some clear indications that a founder is cooking with bacon. (I'm trying to make this phrase a thing—please help me out by using it anytime you want to say "doing a good job.")

Ultimately, as an investor, I want to be afraid. Not for my safety, but afraid that a founder is going to make a huge dent in the universe and I won't be there to help with an investment. What makes me afraid? When that founder shows me a product that's gaining lots of traction (traffic, revenue, or, ideally, both).

I still meet with founders during office hours at cafés across New York City and even at various cafés on my global travels, because I want to give back to the entrepreneurial community that has done so much for me. I also have selfish reasons: as an investor, I want to build a reputation as someone who brings more than a checkbook to a company looking for funding. That said, while twenty minutes' worth of advice and possibly investment will be helpful, the reason the open Internet is such a phenomenal place to operate is that there are no gatekeepers.

You could be told by me, or any other leader in this

industry, that your idea won't work. There's nothing stopping you from proving us wrong. The editor of this book is a gatekeeper whom I managed to win over, and while he has impeccable taste and a winning personality (are you reading this, Rick?), he could've said no to me. But innovation online doesn't have a doorman. The only barriers are an Internet connection, a laptop, and you.

What are you waiting for? Start building. And once you've got something you're pretty sure people want, here's how to take advantage of the world's biggest stage.

You're Introverted? Did Myers or Briggs Tell You That?

They're both wrong. Those Myers-Briggs tests that business schools love are notoriously flawed. In fact, several studies have shown that when people take the test a second time, as many as 50 percent of people will get classified as a different personality—even after only five weeks.[17] By all means take the test, but take it about as seriously as your horoscope. I do not believe we're confined to these slots, although we may have predispositions.

I see personality evolution happen in the span of just a few months at Y Combinator. It takes work, primarily practice, to get up onstage in front of people and pitch. That's why YC insists that founders show up every Tuesday for dinner to pitch to their fellow founders. This has two effects:

17. http://www.indiana.edu/~jobtalk/HRMWebsite/hrm/articles/develop/mbti .pdf

first, it helps people practice the important art of the demo, and in addition, it shames founders into having something new to show every week. If you see your fellow founders every day, it's hard to get a good answer to "What've you been working on?" because it's only been a day. If you haven't got a good answer after a week, something's wrong.

Start pitching. Pitch your cat for practice (they're notoriously hard to impress). The elevator pitch is standard for good reason—you'd better be able to explain your company in an engaging and understandable way within a few sentences—the time it takes to get in the elevator with that potentially life-changing person and successfully pitch her before she gets off at the executive floor.[18]

If you want a stranger to give a damn about what you're working on, you'd better give a damn yourself. Speak sincerely, not like a salesman, and hack away at the words in your pitch until they are as few and as jargon-free as possible. Explain it to the executives like they're five.[19] Well, a precocious five.

Walking and Talking Billboards

I somehow didn't learn that the word *swag* was an acronym until recently—though it's occasionally called schwag (not to be confused with low-grade marijuana). Swag stands for "stuff we all get." If you've been to a conference, you likely

---

18. I would not recommend bringing your cat into a public elevator to practice this part.

19. A nod to one of my favorite subreddits: http://reddit.com/r/explainlikeimfive

ended up with a tote bag full of it: shirts, pins, stress balls, the list goes on and on. It's become an acronym because expectations are so low. There's nothing special when we all get something. T-shirts and stickers are ubiquitous these days, so I'll use the former as an example of how to approach this.

When you hand people a shirt, you're basically asking them to be billboards for you. They're giving up their torsos for your brand, and most people think they're doing you a favor by even allowing you to give them a shirt. And the truth is, they are.

Why do we decide to hang on to shirts years after they've become unfit to wear in public? Sentimental value (and a very tolerant spouse). Your shirt will end up ignored in the closet or in the donation bag unless you can infuse it with some value. A brand people believe in has value, but none of your would-be walking billboards will give a damn about your brand if you don't.

So make swag that people actually want. It's hard enough to get people to be evangelists for your brand, so don't chafe them with a crappy shirt. Once it looks and feels good, make them earn it. I'll coyly tell people who ask for swag to "prove how much you love [insert product name here]." Or I'll surprise customers who've already demonstrated their love—by means of great feedback or lots of activity—with a gift of swag.

If you do it right, you'll give your customer a story to tell when someone asks about the shirt. Now you've got an evangelist. She's going to be the one carrying your brand, feeling sorry for people using your competition, and converting them. She's infinitely more valuable than the billboard on the highway, because she's not doing it for the *money*—she's doing it because she gives a damn.

Here's the good news: if you're making a product or service or idea that people like, this is a tremendous boon. You should certainly do things to encourage your supporters to spread the word. But the future looks far more daunting for the people and companies who dissatisfied and disrespected their customers. The Internet will be their reckoning, because the World Wide Web is flattening the planet. As long as all links are created equal, we have a level playing field—a global platform from which ideas can spread.

CHAPTER FIVE

Startup MBA Part II— Blueprint for Growth

A startup is a company designed to grow fast.... The only essential thing is growth. Everything else we associate with startups follows from growth.

Paul Graham, "Startup = Growth"

Paul Graham, founder of Y Combinator, identifies the core defining characteristic of a startup as growth, which makes it fundamentally different from other types of businesses.[1] No matter how successful a brand-new brick-and-mortar bakery is, it's still not a startup because it's limited by space and muffins and employees, which all require time and capital to grow. I love muffins, but what makes a startup special is that unlike a bakery, it can grow logarithmically (i.e., it can experience hockey-stick growth, up-and-to-the-right growth, and "Holy shit!" growth—okay, I made that last one up). That's because of software. Write the code that solves a real problem and brings in revenue in the process, and investors want to invest in your company—even when it's just two founders in a living room—

---

1. http://paulgraham.com/growth.html

because they know that in a year it could employ fifty people and earn millions in revenue. That's what we're betting on.

The barometer for investors is your startup's growth rate. Keep in mind that the ideal growth rate is measured in revenue, but the alternative metric of active users is typically a good enough proxy. Until you've built something that has traction, you should be checking this rate regularly, probably every week. Don't just count how many new customers you signed up in the last seven days—calculate how many more you signed up this week than last week. Y Combinator says that the ideal growth rate is 5–7 percent per week in the early stages. If you're doing that or better, you're onto something. If not, it's time to reconsider your approach. Until you've found an idea that can generate this kind of growth, raising funding is going to be a feat. So stay cheap (now you know where the phrase "ramen profitable" comes from). Once you've got something that's a proven model and can be turned into an easily replicable (scalable) business, it's time to raise funding and use it to grow the company. In most cases, this involves hiring talent, but in other cases it also entails experimenting with methods of user acquisition (everything from advertising to content creation).

This switch from conservation to investment mode occurs when a startup has found "product market fit" (another bit of jargon, I know, but there's real meat beneath the surface). That's when the magic can happen, because you know you're finally onto something. It certainly doesn't mean your job is done, but it means you've found something that works: you have built a product that people want in a market that's big enough to support it. Common themes emerge when you notice the kinds of founders who get here.

It starts with borderline obsession, both with the problem itself and with the quality of the solution you're building. Plenty of great ideas have been dismissed as awful or crazy or both before the market validated them. Warning: just because your idea has been called awful or crazy or both doesn't mean that it's going to be validated. It means people's opinions won't matter in the face of data showing your idea has genuine traction.

Traction

I'm not a businessman, I'm a business, man.

Jay-Z[2]

You need everyone to believe that what you've made is worth their time. Your mom is the only person who'll blindly think

---

2. From the song "Diamonds from Sierra Leone."

that what you've done is great. The rest of us have a million other things on our minds more important than what you want us to care about, so you've got to show us why we should give a damn. Just don't spam us. Everyone hates spammers. If you've done everything I've suggested in part 1 to build a product people will want to not only use but also talk about, you've built the necessary foundation. I cannot stress this enough: do not take meetings for the sake of taking meetings. Your job is first and foremost to build a business, not to go on coffee dates. The only reason those afore- and soon-to-be-mentioned coffees were so fruitful was because we had already built something people wanted. As a founder, you will always be the face of the company to one degree or another—do it right.

I believe in startup karma. Skeptical? Imagine a reputation score floating above your head. If that's a little too surreal for you, just know that social currency is something you can spend by asking for favors and earn by doing them. Now, even if people aren't actually keeping score (some probably are, but they're the kind of people you should probably avoid), you should always try to keep a positive balance, just as you do in your bank account.

Being the kind of person who's always asking for favors and hustling others is a reputation that not only gets around, it sticks. It'll work in the short term, and perhaps there are some exceptions to the rule who have made it work in the long term, but being someone who's always asking for favors makes the already difficult job of starting something new immeasurably harder.

Instead, look at every meeting as a chance to do someone a solid. This especially matters when dealing with representatives of the media, because just buying them a coffee doesn't mean you're getting a front-page story. Look at every meeting as a long-term investment. She's not writing about your startup? That's okay!

Be helpful. What's she thinking about right now? Some kind of trend is going on in X that's not been covered yet, and she's looking for a founder doing Y. If you can connect the dots, make the introduction for her. You've just helped two people with one e-mail. Cha-ching. More good karma.

Over the years, you can build a reputation as a connector in your field. Connectors are a journalist's trump card when they need to get a lead on an unreported idea, or when they need an introduction in order to land a useful interview. This is a valuable position for you to be in, because it means you're going to stay at the tops of their minds. When your journalist friends are writing about something in your field, whom do you think they're going to reach out to first?

Never Turn Down Cannoli

In between bites of cannolo (yep, that's the singular form of *cannoli*), I was explaining to Rachel Metz, freelance reporter for *Wired*, why reddit.com was going to become the front page of the Internet. She seemed interested, but she could've just been enjoying her cannolo.

I'd taken the Fung Wah bus down from Boston to meet with her in downtown Manhattan because a few weeks earlier, I'd met a friend of hers named Jennifer 8. Lee. Jenny had attended a Halloween party that Steve and I had thrown at our Somerville home and office, and we hit it off. We discussed the subject of her book proposal, which happened to be, of all things, Chinese food. I managed to impress Jenny with my knowledge of Chinese cuisine, so we got to talking that night and that led to her introduction to Rachel.

A few days later, Rachel would confess to me that while she initially wanted to write a story about reddit, she felt we'd become friends and that it wouldn't be professional for her to pursue the story. That was fine by me. No *Wired* story came from that, but I got a new friend in Rachel, one who happened to mention reddit to her editor at *Wired*, Kristen Philipkoski. Kristen, the wife of Kourosh Karimkhany, was doing business development for Condé Nast and heard from Rachel about a pair of plucky founders in Boston working on something interesting called reddit.

And then one day (February 22, 2006, to be precise) this e-mail popped up in my in-box:

> I'm a friend of Rachel Metz. I'm also the director of biz dev for CondéNet, the internet arm of Conde Nast, which, as I'm sure you know, publishes magazines like Wired, GQ, Vogue, New Yorker, Vanity Fair, etc. I'm intrigued with your technology and was hoping to set up a time to talk about possibly working together. I'm open the rest of the day today and Thursday, but will be traveling for a week starting Friday. Do you have time for a phone call? Also, are you based in Boston?

Little did we know that exactly one year after that fateful party on Halloween, Steve and I would be celebrating the acquisition of our company. As if you needed more reasons to throw a Halloween party. Or eat cannoli.

Everyone Is the Media

The traditional public-relations industry model is broken. Good riddance.

The only time I ever wrote a press release was when Condé Nast made me do it for the announcement of our acquisition, and I wasn't about to argue with the company that had just bought my company. But the truth is, I'm not certain that press releases are as relevant as they were in the twentieth century.

These days, everyone you meet is part of the media. Every relationship you enter into, whether it's with a customer or a writer at *The Wall Street Journal*, is a long-term investment. No self-respecting journalist wants to feel like all she does is publish press releases as "news," although some do. The idea that a press release is magically going to compel someone to talk about what you're working on is absurd. At a time when none of us have enough time to pay attention to all the content the Internet produces, you can be sure the professionals who are pitched every minute of the day certainly don't have the spare cycles. This means you're going to have to make yourself known. Here are some things to keep in mind as you do that.

Be Helpful

When you're meeting with a business contact, especially someone who could do you a favor, take the time to learn about that person—even if only to learn how you can be helpful. You won't have any trouble finding the online record of whomever you're looking to pitch—see what she's been writing about and what she's interested in. It could be a commonality that's totally unrelated to your business ("You're also a 'Skins fan, eh? Haven't missed a home game in years, unless I was out of the country") or evidence that she's been following a trend your startup also rides. Just don't you dare make shit up.

If you've been doing your job as a founder, by now you should be an expert in your industry (and maybe even in a few others as well). Use that to your advantage when talking to the media. It gives you insights on bigger trends that are valuable to journalists, so be helpful—even if it's not directly helping you or your company, it is actually still helping you and your company. Anything you can do to help someone else do his or her job better is going to win you that valuable startup karma. Noticing a trend in X meets Y, offer an introduction to some other experts in X meets Y. Be helpful!

While you're at it, you may also be collecting or analyzing a lot of data in your march to expertise. These data are valuable. More and more journalism is trending toward data visualization (think bigger than just infographics), and as we get bombarded with more and more data the ability to separate signal from noise and present it in a compelling, easy-to-digest way becomes ever more valuable. Remember the RentHop team from chapter 4? While Lee Lin was getting his broker's license, he found himself noticing trends. He validated that hunch when he and his co-founder, Lawrence Zhou, started mining mountains of New York rental-price data that revealed everything from how much more people are willing to pay for a doorman to how much less an apartment is worth for every block it sits away from a subway stop. At first, they had no plans to publish any of what they'd learned. Once Lee started promoting RentHop, however, he realized that these data were a tremendous resource. Whether it was a blog post he wrote charting the optimal time of day to search for rentals in New York (spoiler: between 9:00 a.m. and 10:00 a.m.)[3] or a statistic a journalist could cite for an article, it was a piece of added value that bolstered his company's reputation as experts in apartment rentals.

Pitch the Right Journalists the Right Way (by Not Pitching)

Okay, you've found them. Warm introductions to mutual acquaintances from people who know you both well always help, but there's nothing wrong with a cold pitch. Just be concise. I try to write e-mails in fewer than five sentences. Precision with impact is one of the most effective writing skills one can have. The best way to get coverage is to *not* pitch your product. Journalists are human beings. Whether they write for [insert your favorite, most venerable news organization here] or they just launched their first blog yesterday, they do not exist just to write about you or your big idea. Sorry, but it's better you hear it from me now. In order to earn their attention (and their goodwill), you're going to have to give them something. Pitch by not pitching—be helpful. You know what they're into, so send them a link to a breaking yet underreported story you think they'd appreciate. If you can introduce them to a fellow founder who's working in a sector they're covering, offer it to them. Know they love futuristic watches? Let them know when NOOKA

---

3. http://lifehacker.com/5954711/apartment-hunting-heres-the-best -time-of-year-month-and-day-to-search

is having a sale. When and if the time comes to make a pitch (you'll know it when it happens), then do it well.

Tell Stories Around a "Peg"

Pardon the jargon, but it's helpful to know how journalists think. Big trends, things that people are talking about, are "pegs" that you ideally want to anchor to your pitch. It could be as blatant as the Olympics, or it could be more subtle. During the famed billion-dollar acquisition of Instagram by Facebook, Michael Seibel, CEO of SocialCam, a mobile video-sharing app and portfolio company, rode the wave of media attention surrounding the acquisition. It was no surprise that over the next few days, articles buzzed about who would be "Instagram for video." It didn't surprise me one bit when SocialCam was there in every discussion.

Over time you'll develop an eye for it. If you're reading about a particular idea that's got everyone's attention, find a way to connect your own story to it. If you don't get written up, or quoted, or appear to have gotten anything in return for your time, don't fret (and remember what I said about these people not existing to do you a favor). There's always value in taking the time to meet someone. You shouldn't always be pitching, anyway. Build long-term relationships and they'll pay long-term dividends.

Don't Forget to Document Your Startup

Take photos around the office, screenshots of early builds, et cetera. No matter how things turn out, you'll appreciate having these memories later. In the meantime, it'll be useful in a blog post or tweet. And if things turn out really well, people will come to really value those behind-the-scenes photos or embarrassing early builds.

For instance, here's a photo of Steve and me from just days after we'd launched reddit.

Photo courtesy of Trevor Blackwell

Please, please have a decent high-resolution photo of your founders readily available. I've had to arrange last-minute photo shoots for founders who were about to land some great press but didn't have a single decent photo to send. Your smartphone won't cut it. Borrow the nicest digital camera you can find from your nicest friend and take some photos. If nothing else, you can send them to your mom.

For good measure, record the stages of your product, too, even if it's only so you can look back on them with a hearty laugh. No matter how your company turns out, you'll appreciate having a record of its evolution. I use this first version of reddit as an example of just how embarrassed you should be by your first version.

Attentive readers will notice I managed to get –1 karma, because Steve is a jerk.

Once You Get Press, Make a Note of It, Then Get Rid of It

This has been my policy since the day we finally got a taste of attention from the mainstream media. It was a different Internet back then, and it took me months of hustling to finally get someone to write about us. Oddly enough, it was a British newspaper, *The Guardian*, that wrote the first story—six months after we'd launched. It was great to see the increase in our traffic when a digital publication would write about us, but there's something to be said for that palpable version of the news. *The Guardian* kindly sent us a few print copies. I reread the article, imagining better quotes I could've used, and brought it with me on my next trip back home. My parents had hoarded just about everything I did since I was a little kid (only child, remember), and my mom was thrilled to see her son's name in print (I couldn't tell her that it was less exciting than digital, which would have enabled us to actually get click-throughs to our site).

This started a tradition I continue to this day. Even though Mom is gone, I personally send my dad all the press I ever get, because I don't want to see it. I don't want to think about it for more than a day. It's a twenty-four-hour rule. I think I heard a football coach talk about this once in an interview. Feel good about the win for twenty-four hours, and then get your mind off it and think about next week. Same goes for losses, too. But I especially don't want to dwell on past accomplishments, and I recommend the same for my portfolio companies.

Complacency, especially in this industry, is toxic. Remember what I said about your milk shake—forget that kindergarten advice and don't share it.

Spreadsheets Are Your Friends

As a startup founder, you're a cheerleader. You should always have a recent e-mail, or tweet, or quote from one of your users who love you readily at hand. Go a step further and keep a mailing list of those superfans who love you so much they've said they'd be willing to be interviewed about your business. List those people on a spreadsheet that you share among your team, and when you encounter a superfan, ask her if she'd be willing to be contacted by the press at some point and have a testimonial on record.

Each superfan should have his or her own row on your spreadsheet. Establish columns for a favorable quote, home address, occupation, and e-mail address. Always respect a person's privacy and explain why these tidbits are so helpful; years later, when this list gets long and you're trying to help a journalist who's writing about graduate students in the Bronx using [insert your type of product or service here], you can get him connected to the perfect person.

Keep another spreadsheet for press hits, designating columns for important sort criteria like name, e-mail, publication, a pull quote from the piece, and the URL. This becomes your press contacts list. PR people will brag about the size of these as though they were in a locker room, but, as always, it's not about size—it's about how you use it. You're building relationships. It does not matter how many people you have on this list if none of them give a damn about what you have to say.

Start small. As I said earlier, it took six months before any mainstream media wrote an article about us, and until then I was reaching out to anyone who had a blog in tech or media. As you grow beyond your niche, you're going to be forced to connect your idea to bigger trends and find ways to humanize it with real people telling real stories.

Traction starts with a product people want; as word

spreads, you'll start seeing the week-over-week and month-over-month growth that gets investors pulling out their checkbooks and briefcases full of money.[4]

Investment

Summer Camp for Startups

There's an unassuming, slightly bizarre-looking building located at 135 Garden Street in Cambridge, Massachusetts. It's the original home of Y Combinator. When Paul Graham, Jessica Livingston, Dr. Robert Morris, and Trevor Blackwell decided to start a new kind of seed-stage venture capital firm, not many people understood it, let alone expected it to revolutionize tech investment as it has. Today there are scores of Y Combinator clones all over the world, such as TechStars, 500 Startups, and Seedcamp. And I was lucky enough to have been in that first class of founders who showed up for what was then called the Summer Founders Program.

That first class at Y Combinator may have been a special sample of fortunate founders, but the group itself had a range of personalities. There was the braggart, the teacher's pet, even the condescending misanthrope. The one thing we all had in common was that none of us had any idea what we were doing. Some postured better than others, but we were by and large recent college graduates with little or no experience in the professional workforce. Ignorance, in this regard,

---

4. Actually, most investments are done via *duffel bags* full of cash—or via wire transfer.

happens to be one of the best assets founders can have. Living like a college student essentially means being cheap, and being cheap is one of the best ways to not go out of business. If you don't know what you're missing by not having a full-time salary, it's a lot easier to keep eating ramen[5] and picking up leftovers from bakeries at closing time.

Once you've gotten some experience, though, you'll be able to recognize your bad decisions and make better ones the next time. What Paul and the rest of the Y Combinator partners knew was that actually starting a company was going to provide us with a far better education than paying for one at business school would have. Steve and I just couldn't believe we'd be having regular dinners with Paul Graham and a different (impressive) guest each week.

Steve and I showed up early for that first Tuesday dinner at a small building in the quiet suburb of Boston. It was a chance for us to spend some quality time with the partners at Y Combinator as well as with whomever the guest speaker was that week. It was like move-in day all over again, only everyone asked about business models and not hometowns or majors. We gathered around cheese plates, shaking hands and making introductions, before Paul called for everyone's attention. Dinner was served. Crock-Pots bubbled with what would come to be affectionately known as glop. That said, the collection of beans, vegetables, and meats (topped with shredded cheese and/or sour cream!) provided sustenance for our roomful of hungry founders.

---

5. Okay, I have to confess. I didn't eat any ramen during reddit. My low-cost staple was hummus. The Armenian way.

There's a special kind of off-the-record camaraderie that exists within the walls of Y Combinator that allows guests to be far more candid than usual. This means that a roomful of hungry founders (remember, hungry for knowledge, because they're full on glop) can probe the minds of leaders in their industry. Back then Y Combinator was so new that the speaker invite list was limited to Paul's Boston network. But today the likes of Mark Zuckerberg and other famous startup CEOs show up. One of our speakers at that first dinner was a partner at Goodwin Procter, an international law firm, who patiently answered what must have seemed like inane questions from wide-eyed founders who at best had once taken a business law class. Afterward, the speakers lingered, and founders queued to follow up—the law partner not only ended up sticking around and chatting, he would also go on to represent us during our acquisition. He's my personal lawyer to this day.[6]

All of us were there that first summer to learn as much as we could, both from the experts who visited every week for special off-the-record talks and Q&A and from each other. Over time, that network of Y Combinator guests and alums has become one of its strongest assets. At the time, however, not even Paul and the other founders of Y Combinator were aware of the value in the network they were creating. As more founders went through the program, the previous participants felt honor-bound to assist them, a tradition that continues to this day. Encounter a problem you've never experienced before? There's probably someone in the network who has—just ask. It's been referred to as the YC mafia. But

---

6. Note to Mark: If you're reading this, it'd better not count as billable time.

it's not exclusive to Y Combinator. The most healthy startup communities have a network of founders who are genuinely interested in helping one another. I see this today throughout the New York tech community. That level of camaraderie isn't pure altruism; earning "startup karma" means you're more likely to get the help you need when the times comes.

Networks like this don't have to exist within a tech accelerator, but if you can find one that suits both you and your project, you'll likely find many peers there to learn from and share with. Particularly in the Internet industry, there is a strong desire to distribute knowledge, not lock it up. Reputations are built by those who dish out experience and insight. The knowledge sharing happens online—these days within communities like /r/entrepreneur, /r/startups, and Hacker News as well as on Quora and even Twitter. But don't get hung up on the particular platforms of the moment; you can find the discussions wherever they're happening online.

And when they're not happening online, they're happening off-line, at cafés, bars, and work spaces. Even in an increasingly digital world, there's still no replacement for quality face time (never turn down cannoli!). Keep in mind, though: no amount of networking is going to save a website that doesn't actually do something people want.

The phrase "Make something people want" was emblazoned on the shirts each one of us received at the end of that first Y Combinator dinner. Jessica Livingston, one of the YC founders, illustrated this brilliantly in a fundamental way when she taught me people won't wear uncomfortable swag (remember the previous chapter!). As founders, we're never to forget this phrase comfortably adorned on our chests, which serves as a mantra of sorts for Y Combinator. Start-ups will never succeed unless they make something people want. It's a lesson I come back to time and time again.

There's Nothing Fun About Funding

Unless you get incredibly lucky (remember, there are already many factors going against you), you'll need to have at least built something people want before you can get your first round of funding. The application process varies, but most accelerators follow Y Combinator's lead and start with a written application (submitted online, of course) followed by offers for in-person interviews. I'm biased, but not only did Y Combinator create the blueprint, they also set the standard. So at least for as long as they're doing that, let's use them as a benchmark.

If you get in to Y Combinator, you'll trade some equity (typically between 2 percent and 10 percent, but usually between 6 percent and 7 percent) for somewhere around $18,000 (on average) in funding and their three-month program. If you can't ship something in that period, you've got to hard reset.

What if you don't? Or don't want to? Well, you're not alone, as most of the successes in our Internet industry never went through an accelerator.

The cost of starting a company falls every day as the costs of hosting your website fall. When we started reddit, we ordered our servers online, as parts, and assembled them in our living room before schlepping them down to the co-location facility (a big room full of servers where you can rent space to put in your own). Just a few years later, Amazon launched a brilliant cloud computing service that did away with our need to ever see our servers—all it takes is a credit card, and your site can be up and running for a pittance (a price that heads down every month). Hosting a website is now essentially a utility.

When you're not dealing with inventory, or a retail location, the barriers to entry plummet, and businesses can start from dorm rooms and coffee-shop tables. As long as you can cover rent and keep food in your belly, you can keep your business going—and growing—long enough to get that next round of funding.

This funding may come from friends and family, or it may come from wealthy individuals known as angel investors. The phrase is rather generous; I prefer to think of them as wearing monocles and top hats.

The breadpig above captures exactly what I look like at the moment I'm deciding whether or not to invest in a startup. In fact, all investors look exactly like this. No halos or wings, just monocles and top hats.

But the idea is that these investors are willing to take a big chance on a very early-stage company in the hope that they'll get in on the ground floor of something huge. I've done more than sixty of these early-stage investments since selling reddit. For many of us, investing in an early-stage company is a risky investment strategy, but it's something we do because we were entrepreneurs ourselves once. We think of it as startup karma—a way to give back to the community and honor all the folks who took a chance on us.

There are others who invest just because they're fascinated by the industry and can offer some extra insights (this is what people mean when they say they're "value-add investors"—but everyone says that, so you need to figure out specifically what that means). A community of these early-stage investors is important for a startup hub to develop in a particular geographical region, because investment can become a virtuous cycle. Silicon Valley is what it is precisely because of this: some geeks got rich and invested in more geeks, some of whom got rich and did the same. But it's happening all over the world now, and as the costs for starting a company fall, many more companies are getting funding.

It seems obvious, but companies die because they run out of money. Among all the hundreds of startups I've advised over the years, only one has actually been put out of business by a competitor.[7] Despite being in an environment where

---

7. That would be the aforementioned Kiko.com, undone by Gmail's web calendar.

your primary costs fall every day, the leading cause of death for a startup is running out of cash, one would assume that the need to keep costs low is obvious, but it's not.

Additionally, young founders are challenged by a lack of connections and the appearance of youth, which, in many industries, unfortunately, correlates with a lack of legitimacy. Adam Goldstein at hipmunk, then twenty-two, overcame these hurdles through sheer determination. Many other founders do their business development over the phone first, where one is judged only by one's voice and one's choice of words. Then when it comes time for an in-person interview, one's youth becomes an asset, as the executives who would've once been skeptical are now impressed.

Unless you've got a rich and generous uncle, you're going to have to be resourceful. Actually, even with a rich and generous uncle, you'd still better be relentlessly resourceful, because in this industry, if you're not making something people want, you're hosed.

Getting Your Leverage On

Real talk: fund-raising sucks. It's frustrating, and it's a distraction from the most important thing: building your business. But you still have to learn how to do it.

Funding is out there, but most investors are creatures of the herd, sadly. We investors try to tell ourselves we're not, but every founder has been asked, "Who else is in?" There are a few exceptions, but don't count on finding them. Meanwhile, founders are inherently trying to adopt an anti-herd mentality as they build something that solves a problem no one else is seeing. You've no doubt seen the catch-22 here—how does one get investors without an investor?

It's frustrating, but not insurmountable; remember: you're not doing this because it's easy. And when it works, when you do land some solid investors, you can use that social proof to turn the herd mentality to your advantage (just like doing business development in chapter 3). Once investors know they could miss out on the deal, you become infinitely more appealing. A refrain I hear often from founders is "We're closing soon" or "We're oversubscribed, but we're going to try to make room for you." They're trying to create a sense of urgency, and when it's genuine, it's effective at getting me to open my checkbook.

This strategy works because normally investors have the leverage, although that's shifting every day as it keeps getting cheaper to start and grow these startups. But founders still need the capital, and investors want to fund the companies that will win. Showing you're going to be one of those winners with or without an investor's money is a sure way to take back some of that leverage and make him or her want to invest. It'll never completely balance out until you're wealthy enough to fund your own company, and even then you'll likely still want quality investors on your team—but assuming you're still working your way toward obscene wealth, let's take it one step at a time.

Even when you get a commitment, it's not a done deal until the money is in the bank. Never forget the wise words of Paul Graham: "Deals fall through." I've applied it to every deal I've ever done since he first uttered that warning. I even scrawled it on a photo of Paul that I put up in our bathroom after we started talking to Condé Nast about an acquisition. Every day we'd walk in there and see Paul Graham reminding us to stay focused on building a company, not on a potential acquisition deal that could fall through.

How America Gets Her Swagger Back

People are investing in Internet startups even at a time when the US economy is still finding its swagger. Investment capital continues to flow, having faltered only for a brief period after October of 2008, when the bad deeds of the banking community caught up with them (okay, not really; they all did pretty well—some even got great big golden parachutes; it's more like their bad deeds caught up with the rest of us). But now, just like everything else, the investor industry is being disrupted by the Internet.

Innovators Naval Ravikant and Babak Nivi, for example, developed a platform designed to tear down the inefficiencies of angel investing. AngelList is a social network of investors who can share recommendations (or follow the leads of prominent investors) or simply browse seemingly endless pages of profiles of startups seeking funding. A number of companies in my portfolio have been funded this way, including Creative Market and Massive Health, which raised $1.3 million and $2.25 million respectively, thanks to AngelList's seamless network of digital props and connections. It's still not a perfect market, but it's getting better every day. Startups with traction (those that are making money and growing) are having less and less trouble finding funding, whether they're based in the Bay Area, in Brooklyn, or someplace in between.

Once you raise that first round of funding, you'll embark

on the startup "process," which has been charted by none other than Paul Graham in this now-famous traffic graph:

At this point, decisions that were once made with hunches should be made with data (now that you've got a decent sample). Start from there, but also know that even those of us who *know* we're more rational than everyone else are still human. Most decisions still get made on gut instinct—just make sure data is part of the meal before you choose your entrée. Remember: you're not Steve Jobs. And even if you were, you now have real-time data telling you just how good an idea that extra button on the home page is.

You might have the world's best muffin recipe, but as long as you're in the business of baking muffins, your muffinry (that's a bakery that bakes only muffins) will never grow fast enough to be a startup. That's okay, though, because a muffinry can still be a great business. We need more great startups *and* more great businesses.

On that note, the Internet is revolutionizing the way traditional businesses, such as my hypothetical muffinry, get funded (the more I write about it, the more I want to start it). Crowdfunding has hit its stride only in the last few years, with the emergence of sites like Kickstarter (and many, many more in different flavors and for different verticals; see chapter 7), which let anyone with a credit card contribute a reasonable amount of money to a project he or she believes in. For now, investment is technically prohibited (unless you're a rich angel investor), but crowdfunding a project—whether it's a means of taking preorders or simply a means of bringing a dream to fruition—is helping enterprising people help themselves, one small contribution at a time.

These contributions add up. The platform is still young, but there are already examples of projects that have funded companies like Pebble, makers of an innovative new watch that communicates with your smartphone. Pebble had trouble, even after graduating from Y Combinator and after a dogged effort at raising awareness on AngelList—too many investors were worried about hardware startups, reflecting the fact that most investors prefer software, which scales, over anything else. So Pebble began a Kickstarter campaign to fund production of their first batch of watches, aiming to raise one hundred thousand dollars in preorders.

They raised that in mere hours. Once potential customers got a look at their product, everything changed. Granted, these watches look awesome, and the "dream team" they'd assembled was a bright group of Canadians from the University of Waterloo, but even founder Eric Migicovsky was surprised when the campaign raised more than ten million dollars from about sixty-eight thousand people worldwide ($10,266,845, to be exact).[8] They actually capped preorder

---

8. http://www.kickstarter.com/projects/597507018/pebble-e-paper-watch-for-iphone-and-android

requests in order to satisfy expectations, but not before nearly every publication that covers tech or gadgets gushed about their unprecedented Kickstarter campaign.

I know this team well, not only because I was there in the room for their Y Combinator interview but also because I ended up managing the team that does their social media. That started just after their monumental launch on Kickstarter, which shattered all previous fund-raising records for the site—in five days.[9] We watched a global consumer frenzy grow around this product after investors had responded so lukewarmly (remember, even other founders can be wrong). I caught up with Eric months later, when he was in a hiatus between trips to China, where the Pebble watch is manufactured. With the first working prototype on his wrist, the soft-spoken Canadian CEO explained the shock of fund-raising from people around the world, most of whom he didn't know:

> Launching on Kickstarter was the first time we were able to eloquently describe our product to the broader market. We tuned the project page and video until my mom was able to understand the entire thing perfectly. One of the coolest moments was when my friend in Amsterdam saw the page for the first time. All of my friends have been supportive of my work over time, but I knew something was different with Pebble when my friend was telling me to shut up and take his money for Pebble. Then to see the rest of the world think the same was just awesome.

---

9. http://www.wired.com/gadgetlab/2012/04/pebble-smartwatch-breaks -kickstarter-record-in-five-days/

And Pebble won't be the last of its kind. Remember, we're still in the infancy of innovation on the connected Internet, and crowdfunding online still isn't mainstream, even here in the USA.

And as I said at the start: everyone is the media now. Ninety-one people supporting your new restaurant aren't just giving you $15,371 in capital to buy peas and carrots and hire the cooks, as was the case with Colonie, the first Kickstarter-backed restaurant[10] (and one of my neighborhood favorites in Brooklyn Heights). They're giving you publicity: these ninety-one evangelists will spread the word because they feel like the restaurant is theirs, too!

Kickstarter, while it wasn't the first, certainly has been responsible for bringing the notion of web-based crowdfunding to the masses. But this model continues to evolve: it's not the end, it's only the beginning. A few years ago crowdfunding wasn't a proven way to raise money online, but after Eric and his Pebble team raised more than ten million dollars in preorders, people noticed. Now platforms are emerging for scores of verticals. If you need a crowdfunding platform exclusively for [fill in the blank, reader], it probably exists or will be launched by the time you read these words. In fact, that's why I invested in crowdtilt.com, which has built not only a crowdfunding application that lets communities save local toy stores or fraternities fund tailgates, but also the "plumbing" so that anyone can build a crowdfunding application they can dream up using their pipes, so to

---

10. http://www.kickstarter.com/projects/1610300135/brooklyns-cool-colonie-restaurant-coming-soon-to-b?ref=search

speak. What's so exciting is that we're in such new territory. On this battlefield of ideas, there will inevitably be winners and losers, but we'll all be better off for it.

Once crowdfunding proved effective online, technologists and politicians alike (pity there aren't many technologist politicians, but more on that in chapter 8) acted to capitalize on this shift. Yes, even Washington, DC, has been moved to facilitate the innovation made possible by the Internet. In 2012, the JOBS (Jumpstart Our Business Startups) Act passed the House and Senate, and while its ultimate impact remains to be seen, there are already startups pitching investors with the idea that this legislation will next facilitate the iteration of democratizing investment. Their argument goes: If banks won't do it, why don't individuals back our community businesses? I hope the muffin bakers are still reading this. We could all potentially get our morning glories from a cute local bakery that we all own a few dividend-paying shares in. The ideal scenario sounds awfully nice, actually.

The Innovation Multiplier

I'd never heard the phrase "innovation multiplier" until Michael Hancock, mayor of Denver, used it to answer a question I posed to him on a POLITICO panel before the first 2012 presidential debate. It was our first event for the Internet 2012 Bus Tour and I was up way too early. But what he said really struck me, because it set a tone for the rest of our journey through the middle of America. Hancock said that, as startups moved into Denver, the city was experiencing an "innovation multiplier" effect as creative people started building their businesses, bouncing ideas off one another, inspiring more ingenuity, and ultimately generating more innovation. What happens when even one startup takes off is a thing of beauty, because the effect isn't limited to just the startup community where it was launched. In truth, it can affect the success of a muffin bakery in your neighborhood and countless other businesses just like it in other neighborhoods.

So support startups for the muffins' sake. Or if that's not enough, do it for your 'hood.

Why? Because we can't forget what happens in so many of these startup communities once someone has found success. When the founders exit, either through acquisition or an IPO, and when the founders and early employees get rich, many of them will pour money back into the startup economy that raised them. The ecosystem continues to flourish. It's how Silicon Valley got its start, and it's how countless other innovation hubs are developing across the country and around the world. Think of good investors as Yoda firefighters (on call 24-7 to give useful advice or roll up their sleeves and pitch in, although much less heroic) armed with money and talent to help entrepreneurs build businesses, create jobs, and ultimately create more Yoda firefighters, which in turn help entrepreneurs build businesses, create jobs, and…you can probably see where this is going.

"Do or do not…there is no try."[11]

---

11. Yoda, in *Star Wars: Episode V—The Empire Strikes Back* (1980). There's a good chance, based on my reader demographic, that you may not know this movie very well. If you do, you may not even think it's the best one of the series. If that's the case, I implore you to put down this book and go watch it, study it, admire it.

PART III

CHAPTER SIX

Using the Internet's Power to Make the World Suck Less

Do your little bit of good where you are; it's those little bits of good put together that overwhelm the world.

Desmond Tutu

I've given you my own story and my own blueprint, but the promise of the Internet is not just for aspiring entrepreneurs. Entrepreneurial behavior is rewarded online, where traditional gatekeepers don't exist. Even if we're not starting a business, we can use the Internet to leverage human and financial capital—in philanthropy, publishing (both digital and dead-tree), music, and even politics and mass culture— more directly and efficiently than we can anywhere else.

All the people mentioned in the following chapters would have been just as awesome in a less connected world, but we'd probably never have witnessed their talent. What they all have in common is that they didn't ask anyone's permission to strive. Whether you're a public school teacher in Chesapeake, Virginia; a comedian in Austin, Texas; a cartoonist in Tuscaloosa, Alabama; an impoverished soul-music legend in Petaluma, California; or an activist anywhere else in the United States, your time has come today.

When Donors Choose, Students Win

Charles Best was a social studies teacher in the Bronx who, like many of his colleagues, struggled to keep his classroom adequately stocked with school supplies. He and his colleagues, like too many teachers across the United States, were routinely spending up to five hundred dollars of their own money *per year* on supplies for their classrooms. Inspired by this, Charles set out to find a better way. According to Charles, he thought: "I gotta start this site, because if I can tap into the expertise and ideas of my colleagues, we're going to unleash better-targeted, smarter, more awesome ideas than anything that someone's going to come up with at headquarters or in the ivory tower."

Charles had a hunch that there were a lot of people who wanted to help supply underfunded public school classrooms like his, but only if they could easily see where their money was going. Charles set out to build a way for them to verify that their donations were being put to good use. He recognized that these potential small donors wanted to feel like their contributions weren't just going into a black box. Whether they were donating twenty dollars or twenty thousand dollars, they wanted to know that their contributions were making a concrete, measurable difference in the lives of students and teachers. Soon, Charles was hard at work developing a novel way to tap this potentially tremendous resource.

Charles took a simple pencil sketch of his idea to a computer programmer who had recently emigrated from Poland. For two thousand dollars, the programmer built Charles a working version of DonorsChoose.org. This was in 2000, years before anyone was using phrases like "crowdsourcing" or "social media."

The first version of the website was markedly low-tech. Charles used a manual credit-card reader, like the ones you find in grocery stores, to process donations. It wasn't pretty or fast, but it worked. The term "minimum viable product" hadn't been coined yet, but that's exactly what Charles put together. The first projects were posted on the site by Charles and a few of his fellow teachers whom he'd bribed with baked goods from his mother—roasted pears with spices, apricot glaze, and slices of orange rind (remember that part about treating your first customers like gold?).

Those first eleven users then went on to create eleven projects, including a Baby Think It Over doll[1] for health class, quilting supplies for a wall-to-wall art project, and test-prep books for students gearing up for the SAT.

For his own project, Charles, then a history teacher, wanted to fund a field trip for his students to the home of Moctar Teyeb, who'd escaped from modern-day slavery in Mauritania and was then living in the Bronx. Charles had been teaching his students about Frederick Douglass and had told them to read a *New Yorker* profile[2] of Teyeb. With

---

1. A life-size doll that weighs as much as a human baby, cries at 2:00 a.m., and needs to be fed regularly. Imagine a Tamagotchi for high school students.

2. http://www.newyorker.com/archive/2000/01/24/2000_01_24_050_TNY _LIBRY_000020056

the donations from his website, Charles was able to take his class to meet Teyeb in person.

Odds are you're thinking these sound like awesome classroom projects that we'd hope our own children would be fortunate enough to experience. So why wasn't this something the schools themselves could facilitate?

Explains Charles: "It would have taken a huge amount of red tape and waiting, and bureaucracy—and even then good luck—to get the microfunding we needed to execute those ideas." DonorsChoose.org let Charles and his colleagues bypass that red tape. All eleven of the initial projects were funded within days. Charles was onto something.

Today, teachers can request everything from textbooks to microscopes for their classrooms, and donors can read about and even see pictures of their donations in action. That's the connection that motivates people to give to strangers in faraway places. And it works because the story can be told with some easily uploaded photos and some text. The cost to deliver this content is basically zero, and the donation process requires just a credit card. It's not hard to imagine the alternative—a much less effective monthly printed catalog, which of course would quickly become unsustainable given the costs of production.

All the schools and teachers are vetted before they can post projects to the website, and when a project is funded, the teacher doesn't receive cash: she gets the item itself, a transaction facilitated by DonorsChoose.org. On top of that, there's an employee at DonorsChoose.org whose job it is to detect odd activity; she uses data to sniff out suspicious projects and has conducted multiple site visits. More often than not, though, she discovers just another ambitious teacher doing remarkable things to transform a classroom with DonorsChoose.org-funded supplies.

Charles explains, "You could count on one hand, maybe even one or two fingers, the number of projects where something really sketchy happened"—that's out of more than 350,000 projects[3] (at the time of this writing).

Carnegie, Rockefeller, Gates, Buffett, You

DonorsChoose.org has been wildly and consistently successful. Even as institutional donors and school systems have been tightening their purse strings, every year this scrappy nonprofit logs more and more donations to an increasingly wide array of classrooms and projects, Great Recession be damned. In hindsight, this shift toward empowering small donors through transparency and choice seems obvious, but just a few years ago it would have seemed unthinkable (remember, most of the time we don't even realize something is broken until someone else shows us a better way).

When DonorsChoose.org started picking up steam, plenty of traditional foundations weren't fans of this bold new model. "There were foundations that believed that someone, a donor—a citizen philanthropist—wielding nothing more than common sense, not possessed of a PhD or technical expertise, has no business making decisions about which classroom projects are worthiest," says Charles. Even school systems themselves were suspicious: "We had a real cold shoulder

3. http://www.donorschoose.org/about/impact.html

from school system leaders in our first couple years because they thought that teachers were gonna use our site to get funding for books they hadn't approved of, or were gonna get funding to do field trips that deviated from the mandated curriculum."

While some administrators have been wary of DonorsChoose.org, it's been a tremendous hit with its most important beneficiaries: students. Most anyone who's donated through the site can tell you about the awesome feeling that comes with opening an envelope full of handwritten student thank-you notes. There's an immediate connection. You'd be surprised at how thoughtful, passionate, and sometimes funny these thank-you notes can be.

Don't take our word, or the above doodle, as irrefutable proof. Just ask Mudosir, a student in an elementary school classroom whose project I funded. Mudosir sums it up well in a neatly handwritten letter he glued to a fine sheet of purple construction paper and decorated with a bold red crayon border:

Dear Breadpig,

Thank you for the laptops. I love your computers because you can download a lot of games on it. I like the Internet, too, because we were researching for information about plant, animals, and India. Thank you for the laptops. If it wasn't for you we would not have laptops. These are reasons why I want to thank you for the laptops. Thank you very much.

Sincerely,
Mudosir

Now Mudosir has a computer in his classroom that will teach him everything he could want to know about plants, animals, and India. And he's quite thankful for all that.

At the time of this writing, DonorsChoose.org has raised more than $175 million for public schools across the United States. I'm fortunate to sit on the advisory board of this impressive organization, which has made a real impact in the lives of children across the country who need it most.

DonorsChoose.org is the first of several bottom-line-minded, tech-savvy nonprofits to spearhead a massive shift in the way we think about philanthropy, including Kiva .org (I was a volunteer for them in Armenia after my reddit contract ended), Vitanna.org, CharityWater.org, and Global Giving.org, to name a few. I'm convinced this will be the future of giving. No longer will a guilt-inducing letter that arrives in December convince the Internet generation to cut a check for an organization without accountability.

That's the promise of an open Internet. We as donors no longer have to be content with sending our money into a void—we don't want huge percentages of each donation to go to administrative overhead and never reach those who need it. An open Internet connects the once-invisible dots between donors and communities in need, allowing donors and recipients to build strong, transparent connections.

Through DonorsChoose.org, teachers get supplies they need for the education their students deserve (and love); and donors—in a way that feels both personal and substantive—are satisfied knowing their money has actually made the world suck a little less. This is the future of the nonprofit world. If I can see a picture of someone's snack in Amsterdam,[4] I'd better be able to see where my donation is going.

Of all the thousands of projects that DonorsChoose.org has facilitated, perhaps none have had quite the impact of Debby Guardino's.

Joplin

Late in the afternoon on Sunday, May 22, 2011, Joplin, Missouri was hit by an EF5[5] tornado that killed more than 150 people, injured a thousand more, and flat-out obliterated a chunk of this city of about fifty thousand people.[6]

The next morning, the residents surveyed the damage. Among the buildings devastated by the storm was Joplin High School. Although, fortunately, no one was in the school when the storm struck, 260 teachers—many of whom had their own homes damaged or destroyed—were left without classrooms or supplies.

While the residents of Joplin were taking stock of their losses, twelve hundred miles away in Chesapeake, Virginia, a special education teacher named Debby Guardino heard

---

4. *Stroopwafel*, no doubt.

5. EF stands for the Enhanced Fujita Scale, an official rating of a tornado's strength. EF5 is the highest rating on the scale—the same rating given to the tornado featured in the dramatic conclusion of the 1996 film *Twister*. The EF5 that hit Joplin had winds of more than two hundred miles per hour, and it was most definitely not filmed on a Hollywood studio lot using stunt doubles.

6. http://www.usatoday.com/news/nation/2011-05-23-joplin-tornado_n.htm

about the tragedy and was touched. She wanted to do something to help. So she went to her computer.

By her own admission, Debby is hardly a tech expert, but she had been using DonorsChoose.org to solicit donations for supplies in her own classroom. Just a few years ago, this same woman wouldn't have been able to do much more than forward some e-mails to friends. But the modern Internet is one hell of a platform. And Debby Guardino is one hell of a woman. Debby opened DonorsChoose.org in her browser and searched for classroom projects in Joplin, Missouri. Her search returned zero results. Since there were no teachers in Joplin using DonorsChoose.org, Debby started a giving page for them—as anyone who uses the site can do, taking advantage of tools the site freely provides. From there, funds can be raised for whatever classroom projects are posted online.

After she started a giving page, Debby began contacting education companies online—through e-mail, Facebook, Twitter, whatever she could find—asking them to donate supplies she could bring to the Joplin teachers. With no network other than her Internet connection, Debby was able to build momentum for her cause. Among the thousands of people she reached out to were me and the team at hipmunk, who were so moved by her story that we flew her out to Joplin. By the time she arrived in Joplin five weeks later to personally deliver the supplies, she had raised more than four hundred thousand dollars in donations online and had three tractor trailers (seriously, three eighteen-wheelers!) and tons of boxes shipped from all over the country containing educational resources for Joplin teachers. And she did it all from her home in Chesapeake, Virginia, using social media alone.

When Debby arrived in Missouri on July 3, the scene she found was overwhelming:

> Images online do not come close to what it is like on the ground. Try to imagine getting in your car, driving six miles, turning and driving a mile, turn again drive six miles, drive another six miles and then imagine it gone, some areas where I am told there was hundreds of houses, just cement foundations or cellars...and then nothing...no sign that there was anything there...go a little further and parts of houses still standing, but nothing can be salvaged...clothing, toys, furniture crushed in the rubble and items all over the ground... the ground is embedded with fragments of these families' lives...many areas look like the contents of people's homes were churned up like a blender and thrown everywhere... trees stripped of all bark, or pulled up by the roots...but mother nature takes over and these trees that look totally dead...are now sprouting small green leaves.[7]

Debby spent the next twelve days distributing the supplies she'd gathered and showing teachers how to post their own DonorsChoose.org classroom projects online. Amid the work, Debby dashed off another e-mail update for me:

> Tragedy always has a way of revealing human goodness and caring...people here are working around the clock to make

---

7. This is from an e-mail Debby sent me after she arrived in Joplin.

sure teachers are ready for their students to return to school Aug. 17. There is a renewed sense of optimism and just about all of the 260 teachers who lost their classrooms are signed up for donorschoose.org training over the next week and a half.

The connection. It doesn't matter whether it's a connection felt between neighbors working hand in hand to rebuild or a connection between complete strangers joined only by the Internet and their desire to help. Debby said it best: "It makes the world smaller because it makes you believe that people really do care and really do want to help each other."

Debby saw her hard work pay off when schools reopened on schedule on August 12. By that first day of school, she had raised more than eight hundred thousand dollars for 260 teachers. Half of that was raised on DonorsChoose.org within four months of the storm.

It gets even better—the team behind DonorsChoose.org was watching along with the rest of us, cheering her on, supporting her where they could. There were no gatekeepers: not the schools, not the government, not the folks at DonorsChoose.org. When superempowered individuals can take advantage of an online platform like DonorsChoose .org, and when they take advantage of social media—the level playing field that enables everyone to compete for people's attention—they can do big things.

What's so wonderful about this idea is that it's always been anonymous, unheralded individuals who've worked together to bring about great change, yet only recently have we had the tools for them to effectively implement their great ideas at scale.

Success doesn't happen in a vacuum, but the myth is propagated because only a few of us end up in front of the cameras or talking to reporters. Behind Debby Guardino, who is too modest to take half the credit she deserves, were more than five thousand individual donors who gave whatever money they could to her cause—inspired by her and motivated by the ability to effect real change.

With Our Powers Combined

The model developed by Charles Best doesn't apply just to school supplies or computers. The wild success of the crowdfunding site Kickstarter has validated the model and popularized an entirely new way of fund-raising for the masses. But the essence of crowdfunding should be familiar—it connects backers (not donors; in this case, people aren't making a donation but rather a commitment to pay a certain amount for a specified reward as long as the total fund-raising goal is met) with creatives to produce awesome things. Replace "backers" with "donors" and "creatives" with "teachers," and you're rereading the start of this chapter about DonorsChoose.org.

Everything is changing, and no one has a clue what's next or where it's going to end up—and that's why it's so exhilarating. Crowdfunding has given anyone with an Internet connection and a few dollars the chance to support a project he or she believes in. Top hats for everyone!

Well-stocked public school classrooms, startups founded in dorm rooms, creative projects funded by hipsters—these are just a few examples of the things that can become a reality as a result of the Internet's potential for facilitating awesomeness in the world.

I'd like to spend a few moments talking about another crowdfunded project I happen to believe very strongly in. During the 2012 presidential campaign, Erik Martin, general manager of reddit, and I crowdfunded a bus tour across the American heartland so we could meet people and talk about Internet freedom. I'll explore the politics behind this in chapter 8, but for now, know that our goal was to dispel the myth that only Silicon Valley cares about the Internet. We brought a half dozen journalists and our own film crew to record the journey, which became the documentary *Silicon Prairie: America's New Internet Economy.*[8]

Along the way, we met some awesome individuals, including Carl Blake, an Iowa pig farmer who spoke to a crowd at our "Internet Uncaucus" about the fact that crowdfunding platforms like Kickstarter could help him get seed money for his revolutionary ideas in farming, which traditional investors simply wouldn't back. He had plans to use the Internet to circumvent traditional access to capital because it could help his business bring home the bacon.[9] That event was hosted on a bridge that had been closed to traffic, thanks to an Iowa legend, Dwolla, a startup aiming to be the future of online payment. Their network has already transformed businesses large and small—in fact, I even use it to pay my own independent contractors.

We attended a high school football game with the founders of Hudl, a company in Lincoln, Nebraska, that builds software enabling coaches and their athletes to share game footage, and saw firsthand how much of a difference their startup was making.[10] This platform also allows a talented

---

8. You can download it for free! Just for you. Or pay what you want. http://siliconprairiefilm.com

9. Yup, I just did that.

10. Thanks to all the time coaches save by not using archaic methods to edit and share video, they can spend more time with their spouses, and thus Hudl has purportedly even helped save some marriages—although we didn't see that firsthand.

athlete to put together a professional-looking highlight reel, something that would otherwise be nearly impossible for low-income students to afford. These highlight reels can often be very influential when students are applying for athletic scholarships.

Two women, Garnet Griebel and Katie Miller, started Scarlett Garnet jewelry through a relationship that began online. They each found success on Etsy, a marketplace for crafts, which was established in Brooklyn but now connects the world. The site has certainly made a difference in these two women's lives. Scarlett Garnet began as a digital storefront on Etsy and today is a shop in downtown Saint Louis, which we visited when our campaign bus was on the road. Stop by between barbecue tastings if you're in town.

An auditorium full of University of Nebraska students watched me call their congressional representative on speed dial to ask if he supported Internet freedom.[11] I wanted to make sure they all knew just how easy it was (there's an app for that!). A trucker at a rest stop offered to join our convoy once he realized what we were up to. Literally every single person we met—once we explained the half red and half blue bus that had INTERNET 2012 written on it—was excited about our campaign.

Not only did we have a special bus, but the lead car that escorted us on this road trip was built by Local Motors. What's remarkable about these guys isn't just that the car was built entirely in the USA. It's that the design of the car was crowdsourced entirely online. That's right: people from

---

11. His office was closed. I left a polite message.

all over the world contributed designs for a working car that eventually rolled off the assembly line. As a result, the production costs from idea to vroom[12] were a fraction of what it'd cost a traditional auto manufacturer. Also, the entire process happened either in cyberspace or in the United States of America.

The idea for Local Motors came to John "Jay" Rogers while he was a marine serving in Iraq. Frustrated by the inefficient supply line for replacement parts, Jay became convinced there had to be a smarter way to build and maintain vehicles. When he got back to the States he saw the same inefficiencies in the auto industry and realized the old order was long overdue for disruption. So he built a website first, then he built a factory.

At LocalMotors.com, you'll find a community of designers who contribute ideas for every element of the car—from the body to each detail of the interior. All submissions are covered by a Creative Commons license that permits noncommercial use with attribution. Should the company's designers use a community-submitted element, the person who designed it gets paid, but there's more to it than just money. Sangho Kim, the man primarily responsible for designing what became our escort car, was a college student in Pasadena at the time. Kim got twenty thousand dollars in prizes for his contribution, but his work helped get him a job designing for GM Korea. Local Motors built the factory that made the car in the region where it expected to sell the product—a practice known as microfactory retailing—which

---

12. That's an engineering term.

meant that the company's first factory, which produced a desert racer, was built in the American Southwest. From pixels to pavement, this Internet economy knows no bounds.

Whether it's pig farmers in Iowa using a crowdfunding website from New York or an art student in California designing cars for an automaker in Arizona, awesome people are bringing their ideas to fruition using new tools that are emerging all the time. In many cases, these awesome individuals, like Debby Guardino, were able to build great things on the Internet without knowing how to write a line of code. If you've made it here via chapter 5, you know how valuable the ability to develop software is, but it's certainly not a requirement for success online.[13]

One of the lessons of going to the crowd is that it's not just money your contributors give—they're also evangelists who can spread the word about your project and your mission. Just getting someone to try something you've made is a feat unto itself, but to get them to part ways with their hard-earned money is where magic starts happening. A person who gives money to a classroom on DonorsChoose.org or to engineers for a feature on the next Local Motors vehicle is literally *and* figuratively invested in the project and wants to see it succeed because it validates the chance she took. And it feels pretty awesome, too.

These are stories about determined and connected individuals who've inspired and mobilized people because of a technology that closed the gap between inspiration and

---

13. For what it's worth, I haven't written a line of code since a month into reddit, when I quit learning Lisp to focus on all the nontechnical things running reddit required—like doodling custom daily logos.

action. They never needed to ask anyone's permission, and neither did their backers, contributors, and donors. Going online from a computer in Chesapeake, Virginia, or Yerevan, Armenia, has never been so easy or so empowering. And what's more, there are plenty more tools being developed online to help people all over the world, like Debby Guardino and Jay Rogers, identify and solve problems. Want to make the world a better place? Or, as I like to say, just make it suck less? What are you waiting for?

CHAPTER SEVEN

Are You Not Entertained?

The YouTube video opens rather plainly. In a bare room, you see a young man seated in a wheelchair. He has the classic symptoms of cerebral palsy: the lazy eye, the stiff limbs, the halting speech. Immediately you feel a familiar twinge of sympathy. The guy introduces himself as Zach, from Austin, Texas. It's unclear where this is going. He insists that you've met before and that sparks flew, but now it's time you got to know one another better. He's got what he calls "the sexiest of the palsies" and you realize that this isn't going to be like anything you were expecting.

That's how I first met Zach Anner. I met him when so many of his fans did, back when he was just a few hundred pixels tall in our browsers and his video was rocketing up the front page of reddit and very quickly spreading across the Internet. At the time, Oprah Winfrey had launched a competition in which the winner would be rewarded with his or her own talk show on the recently launched Oprah Winfrey Network (OWN). All you had to do was submit a video pitch telling the world why you'd be the next great host. Zach Anner certainly didn't fit the mold of the tradi-tional host, but that's what made so many of us rally behind him. Here was someone who had an original voice and something to say. His video went relatively unnoticed for the first two weeks—until it hit reddit, went viral, and scored a couple million votes.

As usually happens when innovation and corporate sponsorships are involved, though, there was controversy. Zach had a commanding lead until suddenly a number of other contestant videos that weren't even close to Zach's in number of votes jumped to Zach's level or higher. His fans alleged conspiracy—that someone was trying to keep Zach from winning—but OWN insisted they would investigate any impropriety.[1] Regardless, the Internet public wouldn't be thwarted. It was like Mister Splashy Pants all over again. Even John Mayer pitched in, announcing via YouTube that he would write and record a theme song for Zach's show should he win. With the Internet public and the guy who wrote "Your Body Is a Wonderland" on his side, how could Zach lose? Votes poured in for Zach, and ultimately more than nine million people across the country voted to give Zach his own OWN show.[2]

But the competition wasn't over there. When the official numbers came back from OWN, Zach was not in fact among the top five "winners" but was included along with two other "fan favorites."[3] It felt like a bit of a consolation prize—like those "participation trophies" we all got when we were growing up. Along with the nine other winners, he flew

1. http://popwatch.ew.com/2010/06/23/oprah-zach-anner-voting-controversy/

2. http://myown.oprah.com/audition/index.html?request=video_details&response_id=5615

3. http://myown.oprah.com/audition/index.html?request=finalists

out to Harpo Studios to compete in a show about earning a show. How meta.

Zach rolled over the competition all the way to the final elimination round, where it came down to a choice between him and Kristina Kuzmic-Crocco, an effervescent and attractive mom from California who aspired to host her own cooking show. In an oddly anticlimactic move, OWN decided to give both finalists their own shows. It seemed that Zach was finally going to get some of the recognition he deserved. Unfortunately, it quickly became clear that Zach had to do the show his Oprah producers wanted him to do. Even when Zach curbed his creative vision, bigger forces were working against him: OWN was having problems drawing an audience in general, not just an audience for Zach Anner. In the end, *Rollin' with Zach* lasted just four episodes on OWN. Not a single full episode was posted online during its short run. In fact, one can hardly find any of its content, beyond a few teasers, anywhere online even today. For another six months, Zach rolled around Austin and was planning on moving back to his parents' house in Buffalo. Despite having millions of fans around the country, he was now out of work.

That was the state of things when I met him for a giant doughnut at 4:00 a.m. in a cold drizzle under the awning of a church in Round Rock, Texas. After just a brief conversation, I couldn't believe someone this awesome wasn't making a living sharing his unique humor and uncanny affability with the world. Zach remains quite grateful to Oprah, but he was anxious for the chance to make the travel show he *really* wanted to make. In between sugary bites, we plotted his Internet-fueled comeback. Despite the way his show was handled, Zach doesn't hold any grudges. Quite the opposite, actually, because well before Oprah gave him a shot, millions of anonymous people online gave him something better:

> It was the greatest feeling I've ever experienced. Before that, I'm somebody who has a very limited skill set. I'm talented, I know that, but not all the pieces fit. How am I going to make a difference in the world and do something that affects people in a positive way? For the longest time before that audition video blew up, I didn't know if that was possible. I spent a lot of time just banging my head against the wall trying to figure it out. I always used to relate to homeless people, thinking about how easy it would be for me to end up that way if I just don't find a path to make me useful in the world. When that happened, it was the greatest gift because it gave me a way to use what I have and made it clear what my purpose was and why things were the way things were.

Seriously, Someone Else Needs to Drive—He Can't

It's about time we explained that pig with bread wings who's been following us around for the last six chapters. That flying porcine superhero is the mascot for my social enterprise that makes and sells geeky things so that the profits can be donated to charity. It's like a Newman's Own for nerds.[4] None of us at Breadpig had ever produced a show before, and we told Zach Anner as much. But then again, our company had never published a book before *xkcd: volume 0* came out. The point is, if you want to do something awesome, you can find a way. Even book publishing and TV production can be learned with some help along the way. Although we didn't have the technical know-how from day one, we did have something more important: a product that people loved (I trust you remember chapter 5). From there, it was just a matter of finding people with the skills to get our awesome content out into the world.

Our answer, not surprisingly, was the Internet. Video distribution platforms like YouTube and Vimeo have empowered content creators as well as provided them with additional revenue streams through advertising. In only the last few years, global online properties like YouTube and even Amazon have gotten into the content production business. They've built their studio model to be lean, and they make lots of small bets on content that traditional studios simply can't make. They've started writing checks to fund original content that will draw viewers, develop up-and-coming talent, and build the perception that they're not only a place to watch great online video but also a great place to make it. We went to You-

---

4. If you must know, the reason it's called Breadpig is because when Steve and I were settling on a name for reddit, we searched for the word *read* within expired domain listings and found Breadpig.com. Floored by the absurdity of the name, we bought it immediately. Steve envisioned a breadpig as a pig with bread wings, and the rest is history.

Tube first, given Zach's established audience and YouTube presence. All we did was make an introduction. Six months after his show deal fell through, Zach was back in a style befitting the Terminator.[5]

The response from his fans was immediate and clear: "Personal army reporting for duty."[6]

The Internet was thrilled to have him back. Zach found sponsors for *Riding Shotgun* that paid for portions of his production fee in exchange for campy product placements. No one is sure what's next. Zach Anner just wants to make a living entertaining people. He's exploring the possibility

---

5. I hope you remember the opening scene of *The Terminator,* a film robbed by the Academy in 1985, when it was denied the nomination for best picture. In it, time travel is a magical journey one takes (naked) through time and space in an orb of energy.

6. This came from a reddit commenter named DoubleElite. As far as I know, Zach does not in fact have a personal army, but I've also never crossed him.... http://www.reddit.com/r/IAmA/comments/wrf7m/hey_reddit_its_me_zach _anner_remember_when_you/c5fsli1

of a crowdfunded feature-length film. It could be another online series picked up by another production company. What we do know is that his audience grows every day, along with the ways for them to support him. There's a pervasive optimism that spills over from the innovators who build the tools onto all the creatives who use it. As Zach says, "No mountain is too high, and no Atlantis is too underwater or fictional!"

We like to think that real talent always has a way of getting noticed. Harrison Ford was a self-taught professional carpenter when he was hired to build cabinets in the home of George Lucas, who cast him in *American Graffiti* and set him on a course that led to Indiana Jones.[7] If Ford hadn't picked up the right hammer or taken another job, Solo would've ended up saying "I love you, too" instead of "I know."[8] Think about that. There are tons of stories, like Ford's, of extremely talented individuals who couldn't catch a break going through the traditional system, whether in music, film, TV, or publishing. And yet somehow, through connections, or persistence, or pure stupid luck, they get "discovered." This system certainly makes for some romantic stories, but it is actually a terrible business model if what you actually want to do is find smart, talented people and help them make awesome things. The old model probably wouldn't have put Zach Anner on television, no matter how good he might be

---

7. *Inside the Actors Studio*, season 6, episode 13 (August 20, 2000).

8. Seriously. That famous line in *Star Wars: Episode V—The Empire Strikes Back* was total improvisation by Ford.

with a power sander. It certainly wouldn't have given him his own travel show to host. Ironically, an old-style network used the Internet to surface the talent, but they ultimately failed to capitalize on it because they shoehorned Zach into a format—television—where he had neither creative freedom nor an existing coterie of fans.

What's the alternative? It's Zach. It's connecting directly with fans via content you can post online, whether it's a web-comic, a YouTube video, or whatever awesome new thing someone's launching right now. After building an audience, monetize it responsibly, either through traditional means, such as advertising and merchandising, or through platforms that exist solely to fund creative projects. We're witnessing the Internet systematically deconstruct the old apparatus: YouTube for distribution, Kickstarter for financing, scores of options for online advertising. And these are all just a small sample of what's out there and what's to come. In short, there are lots of ways for artists to bypass the old gatekeepers, and more are emerging every day. In light of this, it's also vital to be sure these new media giants don't become new gatekeepers.

Although it's possible for some tastemakers to recognize talent where others don't, the heart of the problem is their inconsistency. It's a bad deal for everyone involved. Back in 1979, a cruelty investigator for a local humane society got the chance to illustrate a weekly comic strip called *Nature's Way* for *The Seattle Times*. He greatly preferred drawing comics to his full-time job, so he got the idea to syndicate his comic. Fortunately, he went on vacation. While in San Francisco, he submitted his comic to the *San Francisco Chronicle* and, luckily, came away with an offer for syndication in some thirty newspapers nationwide. I say "luckily" because when he returned home, *The Seattle Times* canceled his strip—it seemed that some readers found it offensive. Without that offer from the *Chronicle*, he would have "given up cartooning then,"[9] and the world would have never had a chance to meet Gary Larson or *The Far Side*.

Instead of toiling in obscurity at the humane society, Larson created one of the most popular comics of the twentieth century (and a personal favorite of mine). Sometimes things work out. And no success is devoid of some good fortune. It doesn't happen in a vacuum—the open and connected Internet allows unprecedented opportunities for that good luck. I don't want to think of all the Gary Larsons we've missed out on because they never took that fortuitous vacation and were canceled by a gatekeeper before they could share their genius with the world.

Zach Weinersmith

Now I'd like to introduce you to another Zach. Zach Weinersmith[10] has a rich voice, with the gravitas of a man years older than he, and a beautiful, flowing mane of red hair. He's the writer and artist behind *Saturday Morning Breakfast Cereal* (www.smbc-comics.com), one of the most popular webcomics in the world. Hundreds of thousands of people read it

---

9. http://www.salon.com/1999/12/21/larson_2/

10. Born Zach Weiner, he merged names with his wife, the former Kelly Smith, to form the distinguished surname Weinersmith. They're cute like that.

every day—he publishes literally every single day (take that, Sunday newspaper comics section). Also, unlike the Sunday comics standard *The Family Circus*, Zach's series is actually funny.

Zach's work is often compared to Gary Larson's—they're both a smart combination of nerdy and edgy (nerd-gy?). Fortunately for Zach, however, he didn't have to rely on the whims of editors to get his work seen. For the cost of a web domain, Zach was able to get his art up and running. He began publishing in high school, just for fun, but decided after a year of "hating life" in the entertainment industry he wanted comics to be his full-time job. He worked as a closed-captioner to keep paying the bills while he built up his comic, but after two years he had enough revenue from advertising and merchandise to make a living (which he describes as "enough to pay rent and eat some rice"). A year after that, his comic brought in enough to make him "some-what comfortable," which we can only imagine afforded him many bags of rice. Four years after that, he has one of the most popular webcomics in the world and will no longer disclose just how many truckloads of rice he makes per year.

I first learned about Zach's work when his webcomics started appearing regularly on subreddits like /r/funny and /r/comics, long before he spent his days swimming in mountains of rice. It wasn't long thereafter that I offered to be his publisher, as I had with Randall Munroe, author of *xkcd* (another top-tier webcomic with a strange name and loads of readers). In 2011, Breadpig published the first SMBC collection, *Save Yourself, Mammal!*

Courtesy of Zach Weiner

One of the things that really set Zach's books apart was the little doodles he included in the footer on every page. Taken together, they formed a miniature Choose Your Own Adventure–style[11] comic series. It was a thing of genius: he conveyed the intricate decision-making process with just an icon and a bit of text. After the successful run of the second SMBC collection, *The Most Dangerous Game*, which continued Zach's idiosyncratic, footer-based adventure, I pitched Zach

---

11. The original's under copyright.

a crazy idea: an entire Choose Your Own Adventure–type novel.

Like the Choose Your Own Adventure series, it would hinge on Zach's wit and a vast array of magnificent, arbitrary death scenes. When Zach emerged from whatever dark cave he works in, he had *Trial of the Clone*—a futuristic journey starring you, a clone raised by space monks, trying to find your destiny as a hero of the galaxy. As the back cover promises, however, it won't be easy: "Make the wrong decisions and you'll be dead. Really dead. It's hard to emphasize just how dead you will be. So here's a pro tip for you: try to make the right decisions."

Normally, in our role as publisher, Breadpig would front the printing costs, which generally reach the tens of thousands of dollars for a run of ten thousand books. Once we start getting enough revenue to cover our expenses, then we start cutting checks to Zach. That's how it's worked for the last couple of years, anyway. But this is an innovation industry, of course, so that's all changed now.

I'd seen firsthand the power of Kickstarter while running the social side of the Pebble watch campaign, that ten-million-dollar project I referenced in chapter 5. I pitched Zach on doing a Kickstarter campaign for *Trial of the Clone*. Everything was already done: we just needed a compelling video and interesting perks for the various funding levels. We came up with a few straightforward but still worthwhile awards, and Zach recorded a bare-bones pitch video that looks like it was shot in one take with his laptop camera (don't worry, I doubt Zach's reading this). In the video, while Zach reads two books at once, he explains that it's always been his dream to create an adventure-of-your-own-choosing novel. It was simple, and it worked. As an extra incentive for his audience, he added that the money he makes from this book will be given to his wife, Kelly, to fund her research on fish parasites and to advance the study of science. Zach's video didn't require any production team or marketing research (hell, I doubt it took him twenty minutes on his laptop), but he used it to make a connection with hundreds of thousands of strangers.

We knew we'd need about $15,000 for our first production run, so that's where we set the fund-raising goal. Within a few hours we had a good feeling we'd hit our goal, and by day's end, we had. That's when Zach updated backers of the campaign, announcing new rewards if we hit different fund-raising tiers. These included some well-designed surprise perks that would kick in once the crowd had funded the campaign to the fifty-thousand-dollar level. If we hit one hundred thousand dollars, then Zach promised to do a sequel. Gone are the days of "If you build it, hope they'll come."[12] The Internet lets us see if people will come *before* we build it. When they put their hard-earned money down, it's not only getting us closer to paying the balance due, it's also adding more evangelists (think comfy T-shirts).

Zach used all the obvious channels for promoting the book at launch, but most important, he used them afterward to cheer on his backers and even the people who cared

---

12. Imagine if that had been the *Field of Dreams* quote—much less compelling.

enough to spread the word but didn't have any money to spend. He started releasing teaser sections, which became their own "Choosable Path" adventure when he let commenters decide what decisions to make—as a crowd, of course.

This generated more content, which spurred even more discussion about the campaign, and the virtuous cycle of excitement continued to grow as more people learned about this unique novel from Zach Weinersmith. When the campaign ended, Zach had earned $130,132, had sold more than four thousand books directly to his fans, and had promised a sequel. Not too shabby. Six months later, we launched his next book on Kickstarter, a collection of science-related comics called *Science: Ruining Everything Since 1543*, which raised more than one hundred thousand dollars in the first two days. Grow audience; make things they want; sell those things to your audience; repeat.

Lester's Time Has Come Today

This (see photo next page) was the sign Lester Chambers (of the famed 1960s soul group the Chambers Brothers) attached to the gold record that he held in front of his face in a photo seen by millions online. His son, Dylan, first uploaded it to Facebook, and before long it leaped to the top of the /r/music subreddit, where it took off across the web.

One member of the /r/music community, Larakius, had a highly voted comment that sums up how most people felt: "This is why it sickens me when all these record companies

I AM the former Lead Singer of a 60's BAND. I performed before Thousands At Atlanta PoP 2, Miami PoP. NewPort PoP, Atlantic PoP, I did NOT squander my money on drugs oR a Fancy Home. I went from 1967-1994 before I saw my First Royalty Check. The Music Giants I Recorded with only Paid me for 7 of my Albums. I have NEVER seen a Penny in Royalties from my other 10 Albums I Recorded. Our Hit Song was licensed to over 100 Films, T.V. & Commercials WITHOUT our permission. One Major TV Network Used our Song For a National commercial and my Payment was $ 625. dollars. I am Now 72, Trying to live on $ 1200 a Month. Sweet ReliF, a music Charity is taking donations for me. Only the 1 % of Artist can afford to Sue. I AM THE 99%

Courtesy of Dylan Chambers

say 'we need to stop piracy to help the artists. They can barely make a living because of the sheer amount of illegal downloads in today's world.' Greedy fucking bastards."

Another person, astrodust, chimed in with a correction: "By 'help the artists' they mean 'help the company representing the artists get paid.'"

Like many who saw the photo, I was pissed off. There was nothing new about labels taking advantage of artists, but this photo let millions of people online connect with one particular artist's plight. It put a real face on the issue (well, not literally, because Lester's was covered).

Meanwhile, the entertainment industry continues to trumpet its own "important" role in discovering talent and championing the rights of artists (presumably, artists like Lester). If only they spent less time talking about how much they want to help artists and actually did it. Instead, they blame the Internet. I had a chance to debate this matter with Jonathan Taplin, a former manager of the Band and a current professor at the University of Southern California. According to Taplin, the good old days were pretty good; when asked by an audience member about the bad deals bands put together with their labels, Taplin had this to say: "When we had record royalties that were flowing, everybody was making a decent bunch off the master.... When that disappeared [because of music piracy], then the royalties from the records disappeared. And that's the problem."

We were debating at the Innovation Uncensored conference in New York, just months after SOPA's and PIPA's defeat at the hands of millions of Americans who insisted on an open Internet (more about this in chapter 8). Thus I was surprised that anyone from the entertainment industry would come out so soon after the smackdown. It was my first debate. I was nervous, but in a flash that all washed away; that random audience member's question not only reminded me of Lester Chambers, it also suggested a solution that I suddenly felt ballsy enough to propose right on the spot.

Taplin had framed his argument around the tragic circumstances of his good friend Levon Helm, the Band's drummer,
who until a decade ago earned what Taplin called a "decent
living" of a "hundred and fifty, two hundred thousand dollars a year" in royalties. For years, Helm had suffered from
throat cancer, but now, according to Taplin, Helm could no
longer afford his medical bills because of online piracy. Mind
you, the US median household income after inflation was
$50,054[13] at the time, and Helm was making three times that—
paid long after he'd ceased working. A pretty "decent living,"
indeed. But Taplin claimed this all stopped because of piracy.
This is perhaps a better commentary on the national health-
care situation than on the entertainment industry, but in any
case here was an artist—regardless of whether he was a former
millionaire—who was gravely ill. In that split second, I made
a genuine offer there onstage to help promote any creative
project the remaining members of the Band or Helm's family
and friends wanted to do together. I followed the debate with a
more formal open letter, which *Fast Company* published:

> I'm hopeful that innovations like the ones I discussed
> tonight and the others that are being worked on by
> entrepreneurs right now will continue to do right by
> artists and cut out those who'd mistreat them. Please
> take a look around Kickstarter and reddit and you'll
> quickly find that the former is already crowdfunding
> projects in the millions and the latter does not in fact

---

13. http://www.nytimes.com/2012/09/13/us/us-incomes-dropped-last-year
-census-bureau-says.html

hurt artists in any way (quite the opposite, it's full of communities of music makers sharing tips and comedians making oodles by treating their fans respectfully and directly selling them DRM-free content).

Like I said on stage, it would be an honor to gather members of the Band together to produce one more album with unreleased content or something to honor Levon Helm—really any kind of creative project they'd like to produce—(this time funded on Kickstarter) and we'll gladly launch it on the IAmA section of reddit.

I'll have my credit card ready, as I'm sure many other redditors (and music fans) will.[14]

Tragically, Levon Helm died the very next day. As I'd written, I wanted to support some kind of creative project to honor him and at the very least get some funds to his next of kin. No one responded to my offer, but Professor Taplin did reply with an open letter of his own:

"You want to give every great artist a virtual begging bowl with Kickstarter.... Take your charity and shove it. Just let us get paid for our work and stop deciding that you can unilaterally make it free."[15]

The problem with Taplin's argument, of course, is that helping artists get paid for their work, directly by their fans, is precisely what the Internet makes possible. I wish I had the power Professor Taplin implies I have, but I don't. The

---

14. http://www.fastcompany.com/1834666/reddit-founder-alexis-ohanians -open-letter-about-music-industry-and-band

15. http://www.fastcompany.com/1834866/bands-ex-tour-manager -blasts-reddit-founder-alexis-ohanian-kim-dotcom-kickstarter-begging-bo

digital revolution changed the game, and most of us—from artists to fans to entrepreneurs—understand the shift and are adapting. Kickstarter happens to be one example of a great new innovation, but, as I've said, it's only one of many and just the beginning of what will, I hope, be decades of improvement.

Months went by as we got caught up launching *Trial of the Clone*, the adventure-of-your-own-choosing novel by Zach Weinersmith I mentioned earlier. But I kept returning to this idea of a fund-raiser for Lester. Talking about a solution isn't nearly as compelling as doing it, after all. And I love doing things.

Fortunately, in 2012 Lester and I didn't have to ask anyone's permission to produce a new album wholly owned by Lester Chambers himself. Breadpig would help him produce it, but our corporate aim wouldn't be to make any money for ourselves—it would be to make the world suck less. Lester, the artist doing most of the work, would control the project and the profits. Our only request was that he pay it forward, which he happily agreed to. A percentage of the profits from his Kickstarter account would go to help other artists like him through the Sweet Relief Musicians Fund, a nonprofit agency. Before we get into that, though, I want to share a little more of Lester's story with you.

"We Trusted People Too Much"

John Hammond Jr., carrying only a guitar and a sack of clothes, had been traveling the country when he wandered into Santa Monica and met the Chambers Brothers, who took him in. Turned out his father, John Hammond Sr., was a Columbia Records producer (note again the serendipity business model in full swing).

Bob Dylan had asked the Chambers Brothers to do background vocals on "Tombstone Blues," a song on the album *Highway 61 Revisited*, which they were thrilled to do. But it turned out they were too good—they outshone Bob's voice—so they were asked to come by Hammond Sr.'s office after the recording was complete. He offered them a contract with Columbia Records. For a moment, it seemed like fame and fortune were just a step away for the four young brothers from Mississippi. Hammond was on his way out of the company, but he told the brothers he wanted them to sign a contract anyway.

But they never got a producer. They were shelved. The reasons weren't very good—apparently Columbia Records had another group, Paul Revere and the Raiders, that they wanted to promote instead. At least that's what they told Lester and his brothers.

Fortunately, another producer, David Rubinson, stepped in and told the band they were too good to be ignored. He wanted to see their album get made and talked the brothers into getting it made without a producer. "We did the album for less than twelve thousand dollars," says Lester. Thankfully, Lester had arranged a trip to Boston, where a gig led to their album finally hitting the shelves.

"We had developed such an audience that they heard about this record being out and we told the guy who owned the record store in Cambridge that we had the record out." He had no idea they even had an album and ordered fifty thousand records. They sold out in a few hours.

"Gone. Completely sold out. He was the first guy to sell the record."

Sold-out shows. Despite a total lack of interest from their record company, fans found a way to connect with the Chambers Brothers. But how'd that record store owner in Massachusetts hear about them? Alas, I know the answer to this question isn't /r/music, which would be as awesome as it'd be anachronistic.

The owner had seen the group selling out night after night and had seen lines of devoted fans braving rainstorms for a chance to hear the Chambers Brothers play. It all starts coming into focus. The same way the Internet displays fan demand, live concerts allowed this one record store owner in Cambridge, Massachusetts, to see consumer demand right in front of his eyes.

"We had the audience. There was no way the record couldn't be sold."

Needless to say things got a bit awkward when the Chambers Brothers found themselves back at Columbia Records headquarters accepting their gold record (the one Lester held up in the viral photo)—the record they earned in spite of all the "support" their production company had given them.

Despite the Chambers Brothers' success, their label didn't show them a lot of love, to say the least. According to Lester, "We never got promoted once. Columbia Records sent us to do a promotional tour…they said you are to go and sing at this mall, or this store, and give records away. That was the way they promoted us."

That's right: the same industry whose leadership was "astounded at the entitlement that people felt to get their music for free"[16] was literally giving away records back in 1966. And they did little to promote the group's appearances at these record-giveaway events. Despite that, Lester and his brothers slowly kept getting recognition. "We had top ten, top three, all over the world."

Lester doesn't mince words about the experience. "In my mind, the record companies are the worst sharecroppers in the world." (Lester and his brothers grew up in rural Mississippi in the 1940s.)

Even after everything that's happened to him, he's got two good reasons to be optimistic, one timely and the other timeless.

"You don't really need a record company anymore. You don't really need a distributor anymore." You'd think Lester Chambers was onstage pitching his music startup at a tech conference. Then a serious expression comes over his face. This is not going to be about "synergy."

"My son, Michael Dylan, said, 'Dad, don't worry. I'm never gonna leave you. I'll always stay by your side.' He slept on the floor with me.... Every father in the world should have a son like I have."

Even with a daunting list of illnesses and a life of hardship in the music industry, Lester is not a beaten man—far from it. It's clear that his son is a big part of that.

When I tell Lester about Kickstarter and the idea of crowdfunding his own album, his eyes light up. His fans old and new would be able to fund his project by preordering digital downloads, or signed CDs, or even autographed cowbells.

---

16. http://www.vice.com/read/downloading-some-bullshit-484-v17n8

There wouldn't be any labels or record company contracts. Just an artist getting paid by for his work by his fans. After all, isn't that what Professor Taplin said he wanted, too?

Looking back on it, Lester says the record labels were always the thing getting between artists and their fans. I asked him what the opportunity to have a direct connection with his fans through the Internet meant to him. "Oh, God, you just don't know. I'm wide open. Call me. E-mail me. I'll get back to you—promise. It's so great to be able to communicate with your audience worldwide."

By connecting with his fans through the Internet, Lester won't have to give any of his profits to middlemen. And he won't have to ask anyone's permission.

Internet Rights and the Wrongs of the Music Industry

A decade ago, Cary Sherman, head of the RIAA (Recording Industry Association of America), was asked if the RIAA was now obsolete, thanks to the advent of digital distribution. "We have no problem with a music industry that is more diversified, that gives new opportunities for new labels and new artists," he said.[17] To his credit, Sherman has reached the acceptance stage regarding the inevitability of the Internet era. He goes on: "This is not about maintaining control; it's about being fair in regards to the ability of people to get paid for their work."

Lester clearly disagrees. Fortunately, we can take the

---

17. http://pcworld.about.net/news/Oct302003id113133.htm

matter into our own hands and launch our own online campaign called Lester's Time Has Come Today, and we launched it on December 10, 2012. The first week was slow, and we'd only raised $10,000 of Lester's budgeted $39,000 goal, which would cover the entire production of the album, payment for band members, and fulfillment of the various rewards, such as T-shirts and even signed cowbells. Turns out I'd forgotten to upload the trailer to YouTube: I'd only uploaded it to Kickstarter, where it couldn't be as easily shared. My bad. As soon as my foolishness was corrected, we raised more than $18,000 in a single day as the video blazed around the social web. This buzz triggered attention from bloggers, who covered the story, which eventually connected us to a writer at CNN, who wanted to write an article for the website. We still had five thousand dollars to go when that story hit the front page of CNN.com and stayed there for most of Christmas Eve—Dylan and Lester grinning for all the world to see.

The next morning father and son were interviewed on the CNN show *Starting Point*. Boom. That put us over the top. Way over.

When the project ended, we'd nearly doubled our goal, and Lester had $61,084—minus a few percentage points in fees to Kickstarter and credit card companies—to make his record and reward his fans. And this time, it was all going to belong to him. It made me so proud to finally say, "Lester, your time has come today."

The industry of art, like other industries, is dramatically changing, thanks to the open Internet. For some time, only a few fortunate individuals who had wealthy patrons were able to produce art. But today, the social web has made it possible for any artist with a good idea and an Internet connection to create, publicize, and monetize his art. As power shifts from incumbents trying to preserve outdated business models to newly empowered artists, it's bound to make former gatekeepers uncomfortable, even scared. That's usually a positive sign. We'll be able to enjoy the work of comedians, cartoonists, and musicians who otherwise would've come and gone without ever sharing their genius with the world. And the best part is that everything I've mentioned so far has happened only during the last decade. It's just the beginning. Where will we discover the next Zach Anner? Where will the next Zach Weinersmith find an audience for his art? Where will the next Lester Chambers get his due? My money is on the open Internet.

CHAPTER EIGHT

Mr. Ohanian Goes to Washington

It has been said that democracy is the worst form of government except all the others that have been tried.
Winston Churchill

It was supposed to be a vacation. And not just a normal vacation—a once-in-a-lifetime birthday surprise for my girl-friend, Sabriya. A week and change at a rented house in the West Indies with me and her closest friends. I don't take many (any?) vacations, but this was going to be something special. I'd been surreptitiously planning it for almost a year. Somehow, I'd managed to keep the part about her friends a secret until we were on the plane, which we boarded last to ensure that she'd see all her friends at once, waving from their seats, as we all sang "Happy Birthday" to her. I even coaxed the flight attendants to sing along over the PA.[1]

At that moment, standing in the aisle of our JetBlue plane, I was just happy to see her crying tears of joy as she realized she wasn't going to be stuck with just me during

---

1. In retrospect, I think I owe someone an apology.

her week in paradise—she'd also be with other people who loved her. It turned out to be a good thing they were there, too, because halfway into that trip I'd get an e-mail about another, decidedly less sexy trip I'd be taking when I got back. Rather than relaxing with my girlfriend on the beach, I'd be thinking about Washington, DC, the House of Representatives, and the written and oral testimony I was scheduled to deliver a few days later.

How the House of Representatives Ruined My Vacation

Let me wind back just a moment. Recall that just five months earlier I'd found myself suddenly unemployed (remember the end of chapter 4?). Without a startup to run or cute mascots to draw, I focused on a number of projects involving my social enterprise, Breadpig.

Then, on November 6, 2011, I got an e-mail from Christina Xu, one of my co-workers at Breadpig. The subject of the e-mail was two pieces of pending legislation—SOPA and PIPA—and a day of protests that some of Christina's friends were organizing online. The date of the protests, which they were calling Internet Censorship Day, struck me. It was November 16, which would have been my mom's fifty-eighth birthday.

Before that day, I'd never had an interest in politics. I always believed I could do more to make the world suck less in the private sector, which is why I've never left it. In the Internet industry, we're used to ideas winning just because they're better. On an open Internet, where all links are created equal, as you know, you win by building something people want. And as you've seen throughout this book, it doesn't matter if it's a nonprofit or a for-profit or a music album or a travel show—the rule applies everywhere online.

SOPA and PIPA threatened to change all that. The result of intense[2] lobbying by the entertainment industry, the Stop Online Piracy Act (SOPA) and PROTECT IP Act (PIPA) were so technically stupid that they could have been written only by K Street consultants and pitched as a bipartisan solution to a nonexistent problem so that the members of one of the least productive Congresses in history[3] could claim at least *some* kind of accomplishment during their reelection campaigns. It would have been a nice little holiday show of cooperation that would have ruined the Internet under the guise of protecting copyright. Quite an awful stocking stuffer from Congress.

These bills were marketed as a solution to Internet piracy, but in fact they wouldn't have curbed piracy. Rather, they would've only curbed First Amendment rights online while simultaneously stifling American job growth. But don't take my word for it—ask renowned constitutional scholar Laurence Tribe, who wrote an open letter to Congress denouncing SOPA for its First Amendment violations:[4]

---

2. As in $94 million in 2011 alone: http://www.politico.com/news/stories/1111/68448_Page4.html

3. http://www.nytimes.com/2012/09/19/us/politics/congress-nears-end-of-least-productive-session.html?_r=0

4. http://www.scribd.com/doc/75153093/Tribe-Legis-Memo-on-SOPA-12-6-11-1

Although SOPA's supporters have described the bill as directed at "foreign rogue websites," the definitions in the bill are not in fact limited to foreign sites or to sites engaged in egregious piracy. SOPA will lead to the silencing of a vast swath of fully protected speech and to the shutdown of sites that have not themselves violated any copyright or trademark laws.

That's a pretty serious violation of the First Amendment's prohibition of prior restraint—that is, prohibition of censorship—according to Tribe. Basically, it means that private parties (e.g., entertainment megaliths) would have had the ability to shut down businesses that American companies—for example, advertisers and credit card providers—conduct with alleged "pirate" websites simply by filing a notice, without prior notification and without a judicial hearing. Once again: that means that SOPA would have delegated the power to suppress First Amendment rights to private corporations.

What that means in practice is that American website owners, founders like me and Steve, would have needed a lot more than just a laptop and an Internet connection to get started and be competitive. Steve and I would've needed a team of lawyers and people policing reddit 24-7. Basically, we would have needed to have been a giant entertainment company. Not only is this extremely anticompetitive, it's also extremely anti-innovative. Tribe again lays out why this would have been so awful for anyone trying to build a social media platform or run any website with user-generated content, even a blog that allows user comments. If this bill had become law, you could've thrown out every single previous chapter in this book. If this bill had been law back in 2005, when I graduated from UVA, there'd have been no book to write. Here's Tribe again:

> SOPA provides that a complaining party can file a notice alleging that it is harmed by the activities occurring on the site "or portion thereof." Conceivably, an entire website containing tens of thousands of pages could be targeted if only a single page were accused of infringement. Such an approach would create severe practical problems for sites with substantial user-generated content, such as Facebook, Twitter, and YouTube, and for blogs that allow users to post videos, photos, and other materials.

Furthermore, SOPA defined a "domestic Internet site" as having a "domestic domain name" and a "foreign Internet site" as "not a domestic Internet site." The absurdity of this becomes pretty clear when one realizes how many US Internet companies use nondomestic domain names— even reddit uses the Italian "redd.it" as our URL shortener. Under SOPA, that would have made reddit a "foreign Internet site."

Think that's dumb? It gets worse: plenty of foreign-run websites use "domestic" domain names like .com, which, according to SOPA, would qualify them as domestic Internet sites even if they're run from Albania.

Despite lots of crowing to the contrary, these weren't minor concerns that might've been smoothed out after the bills were implemented. As Tribe says:

It is a blunderbuss rather than a properly limited response, and its stiff penalties would significantly endanger legitimate websites and services. Its constitutional defects are not marginal ones that could readily be trimmed in the process of applying and enforcing it in particular cases. Rather, its very existence would dramatically chill protected speech by undermining the openness and free exchange of information at the heart of the Internet. It should not be enacted by Congress.

The bills demonstrated a complete lack of understanding of the Internet. You'd think with the $94 million the entertainment industry spent lobbying Congress that year the lobbyists they hired could've taken the time to google how the Internet works. Instead, Congress and the entertainment industry were poised to pass legislation that threatened not only my livelihood but also the health and future of innovation in America. So on November 17,[5] I joined a diverse group of Internet experts in Washington, DC—folks like Micah Schaffer, who was one of the first hires at YouTube and responsible for handling copyright enforcement, and Christian Dawson, who ran ServInt, an Internet service provider in Virginia. We were all there, in suits, for a series of meetings with congressional representatives, led by Michael Petricone of Consumer Electronics Association.

---

5. https://plus.google.com/113164038788726940319/posts/ab9eFgmovJ1

Good Thing I Knew How to Tie a Tie

When we got to Capitol Hill to make our case, no one in Washington thought we had a chance. I loved those odds. Five of us in business attire visited one office after another, meeting staff and sometimes the senator or representative him- or herself. Each visit followed a similar pattern: after being greeted and welcomed into the meeting room, we were given a few minutes each to speak our minds as we went around the table. I had about 240 seconds to make an impact.

The night before, I'd asked /r/technology, a subreddit for fans of—you guessed it—technology, what I should focus on. Should I talk about how my entrepreneurial story couldn't have happened if SOPA and/or PIPA were enacted into law, or should I talk about how these laws could be used as an excuse for censorship?

A redditor with the handle fangolo got right to the point: "Say 'job killing' at least three times. Seriously."

Another, StoicBuddha, who claims to be a former congressional staffer, elaborated:

> So in order to convince them, you have to frame the debate in terms of how SOPA affects those two things [entrepreneurship and censorship]. Posting news clips of themselves helps them demonstrate to their constituents what a good job they're doing. Pointing [out] how this would be breaking the law takes the debate out of technical and legal mumbo jumbo and frame[s] it in a way that they can directly relate [to]. The more

examples like this you can provide, the better. Given the choice between standing up against censorship and getting reelected, they'll choose the latter every time.

The decision was obvious. I had the benefit of a few hundred thousand people reading and voting on suggestions, enabling me to craft the perfect pitch with the help of the ultimate "focus group." I took this feedback to heart and rehearsed, getting my elevator pitch as concise as possible, just as if I were pitching to investors back in my previous life as a founder.

This time, though, the stakes were far higher—being turned down for funding isn't the end of a startup (it's just part of the life). But if either of these bills had passed the House or Senate, it would've stopped countless would-be founders from pursuing their dreams and would've robbed the rest of us of all the great things they might've brought into the world.

So with sweaty palms I told my story. I explained how Steve Huffman and I started with less money than it takes to buy a new Ford Focus and built a company that made us millionaires two years later and founders of one of the world's most popular websites five years later. We were fortunate enough to live the American dream online, and that simply couldn't have happened in a world with SOPA or PIPA in it.

In nearly every case, that got their attention.

As we left the Hill, we knew there was much more work left to be done, but we had reason to be a little more optimistic. By day's end, Senator Jerry Moran (R-Kansas), one of the legislators we met, signed on to a statement against the PROTECT IP Act, saying, "We take seriously the alarm expressed by the nation's leading investors in new online startups who say the proposal will dampen interest in financing the new ideas and businesses of tomorrow."

Bring In the Nerds

I almost didn't make it to the last meeting, which was with a Republican representative from Utah, Jason Chaffetz, but I'm glad I did. He admitted up front that he wasn't a technologist, but also that he was very interested in understanding our technological arguments against the legislation. He was attentive as we went around the table, and he listened to each of us as we brought our different perspectives to bear on our common argument. Before I knew it, the meeting had ended, and we were all posing for a photo.

Our visit to Mr. Chaffetz's office paid off, because he proved to be one of the few rational voices in the House Judiciary Committee meeting that debated the issue:[6]

> We're going to do surgery on the Internet and we haven't had a doctor in the room to tell us how we're going to change these organs. We're basically gonna reconfigure the Internet and how it's gonna work without bringing in the nerds....I worry that we did not take the time to have a hearing to truly understand what it is we're doing.

Mr. Chaffetz and the House of Representatives were the furthest things from my mind while I was relaxing with my

---

6. http://www.youtube.com/watch?v=xrrj9Wc2L84

girlfriend on the beach, but it was Mr. Chaffetz's comments that led to another fateful e-mail. It came from someone in the office of Darrell Issa (R-California), chairman of the House Committee on Oversight and Government Reform. The e-mail itself was a pretty simple press release:

ISSA ANNOUNCES OVERSIGHT HEARING ON DNS & SEARCH ENGINE BLOCKING

WASHINGTON, DC—House Committee on Oversight and Government Reform Chairman Darrell Issa (R-CA) today announced that the Full Committee will hold a hearing on January 18 to examine the potential impact of Domain Name Service (DNS) and search engine blocking on American cyber-security, jobs and the Internet community. In light of policy proposals affecting the way taxpayers access the Internet, the hearing will also explore federal government strategies to protect American intellectual property without adversely affecting economic growth. The Committee will hear testimony from top cyber-security experts and technology job creators.

"An open Internet is crucial to American job creation, government operations, and the daily routines of Americans from all walks of life," said Issa. "The public deserves a full discussion about the consequences of changing the way Americans access information and communicate on the Internet today."

WITNESSES
Mr. Stewart Baker: Partner, Steptoe & Johnson LLP
Mr. Brad Burnham: Partner, Union Square Ventures

Mr. Daniel Kaminsky: Security Researcher and Fortune 500 Advisor

Mr. Michael Macleod-Ball: Chief of Staff/First Amendment Counsel, American Civil Liberties Union

Mr. Lanham Napier: Chief Executive Officer, Rackspace Hosting

Dr. Leonard Napolitano: Director, Center for Computer Sciences & Information Technology Sandia National Laboratories

Mr. Alexis Ohanian: Co-Founder, Reddit.com, and Web Entrepreneur

There I was, along with six other expert nerds. In just over a week, we would be testifying before Congress.

Meanwhile, on the Internet...

Of course, I wasn't the only one up in arms about SOPA and PIPA—far from it. Across the web, millions of people—a few famous, but most of them not; some using their real names, others anonymous—were furiously working to spread the word about these bills and coordinate a response that would get the attention of lawmakers. Months of action online and extensive social media chatter led up to a day of protest on January 18, 2012. The impact of this off-line and online protest was unlike anything seen before in the United States. Fifteen years earlier, the US Supreme Court talked about the potential for anyone using the Internet to "become a town crier with a voice that resonates farther than it could from any soapbox," but until this watershed moment, we'd never seen that voice actually resonate among millions of people.[7] The social web changed that, and the defeat of SOPA and PIPA was, poetically, enabled by the very technology those bills threatened.

Israeli-American legal scholar Yochai Benkler researched what he calls the "networked public sphere" using eighteen months of text and link analysis to identify the most-linked-to online sources as the voice of the "town crier" resonated across the web.[8] At this point it shouldn't surprise you that there wasn't just one source, but rather a chorus. It all started on September 20, 2010—which, if you're keeping track, is more than a year before I even got involved—with an article in *The Hill* about a "bipartisan bill" called COICA (Combating Online Infringement and Counterfeits Act).[9] Just three days later, it'd be up for a vote—a curiously quick process—and with bipartisan support from members of the Senate Judiciary Committee it looked like a done deal.

Early attention to this bill came largely from the tech press—both mainstream publications, such as Wired.com, and niche publications, such as techdirt.com—and from nonprofits, such as the Electronic Frontier Foundation, which was railing against the bill, and Demand Progress, which was gathering signatures on a petition against it. Unfortunately, the bill passed the Senate Judiciary Committee—unanimously.

---

7. https://bulk.resource.org/courts.gov/c/US/521/521.US.844.96-511.html

8. http://www.guardian.co.uk/media-network/video/2012/may/15/yochai-benkler
-networked-public-sphere-sopa-pipa

9. http://thehill.com/blogs/hillicon-valley/technology/119771-bipartisan-bill
-would-ramp-up-anti-piracy-enforcement-online

Now imagine this part in slow motion with dramatic music playing in the background: Senator Ron Wyden (D-Oregon) put a hold on the bill, saying, "The collateral damage of this statute could be American innovation, American jobs, and a secure Internet."[10] Epic. The bill was not gone, however. A year later it returned—still awful—with a new name: the PROTECT IP Act (PIPA). The Stop Online Piracy Act (SOPA) would follow in the House. Fortunately for us, when it comes to the speed of innovation, that's a long time in Internet years.

As Yochai Benkler's research shows, Senator Wyden declared in a widely linked release in May of 2011 that he would also place a hold on this new bill. But this release also served as a call to the Internet public for help.[11] Content began to surface and websites emerged that called for even more action. One of these sites, AmericanCensorship .org, was organized by the group Fight for the Future, which proved to be a powerful mobilizing force in the months that followed. All the while attention was coming from across the political spectrum, from Pajamas Media (right-leaning) to the Democratic Underground (left-leaning) to the venture capital community (Fred Wilson at Union Square Ventures). People weren't linking just for information; they were linking to take action.

On December 21, the Judiciary Committee named all the corporate supporters of these bills. The next day, a redditor named selfprodigy suggested that people boycott one of those

---

10. http://arstechnica.com/tech-policy/2010/11/senator-web-censorship-bill-a -bunker-busting-cluster-bomb/

11. http://www.wyden.senate.gov/news/press-releases/wyden-places -hold-on-protect-ip-act

companies, GoDaddy, a popular domain-name registrar known for its tacky television commercials and even worse taste in legislation.[12] The boycott went viral within hours.

Later that same day, GoDaddy withdrew its support for the bills.[13]

That early taste of success emboldened us even more. Early in the new year, moderators of popular subreddits discussed blacking out for a day in protest of SOPA and PIPA.[14] More and more moderators signed on until eventually the reddit administrative team decided to take down the entire website for twelve hours on January 18.[15] Instead of the usual list of top links, millions of visitors would be greeted with a short explanation about SOPA, PIPA, the blackout, and what they could do to help.

This started a chain reaction among other sites that culminated a week later, when the Wikipedia community voted to go dark for the day as well.[16] Suddenly the blackout was everywhere. Even Google agreed to censor their logo and offered visitors a chance to learn about the digital protest. All told, most of the biggest names in the Internet economy did something in protest: Wikipedia, Google, Mozilla, Tumblr, WordPress, Fark, Cheezburger, Imgur, and, of course, reddit, to name just a few.

---

12. http://www.reddit.com/r/politics/comments/nmnie/godaddy_supports _sopa_im_transferring_51_domains/

13. http://support.godaddy.com/godaddy/go-daddys-position-on-sopa/

14. http://www.reddit.com/r/AskReddit/comments/o7ch9/lets_discuss_sopa _askreddit/

15. http://blog.reddit.com/2012/01/stopped-they-must-be-on-this-all.html

16. http://en.wikipedia.org/wiki/Wikipedia:SOPA_initiative/Action

But it wasn't just about the dot-com startups. Hundreds of webcomics, including *xkcd*, *The Oatmeal*, *Dinosaur Comics*, *Cyanide & Happiness*, and Zach Weinersmith's *Saturday Morning Breakfast Cereal* (from chapter 7), agreed to black out together in solidarity. The artists behind these comics made their living thanks to an open Internet. Thousands of other websites, large and small, from craigslist to mommy bloggers—even the iSchool at Syracuse University—all pledged to join together in a day of blackout.

Social media has made huge strides in terms of changing the way we hear about and spread the news. For Washington lawmakers who may not "do e-mail," however, nothing beats hearing your message from an anchor on CNN or Fox News.

While I'm quite proud of reddit for being the first to black out, it was Wikipedia's participation that forced the mainstream media to pay attention. Until Wikipedia announced it was joining in the blackouts, the major television networks (MSNBC, Fox News, ABC, CBS, and NBC) had basically ignored both bills during their evening broadcasts. One network, CNN, devoted a single evening segment to it, but that was it.[17] The reason was pretty straightforward. As David Carr of *The New York Times*[18] wrote:

17. In their defense, Bloomberg TV invited me to talk about the bills on January 5. It may have been an audience of day traders and bankers, but it was an audience nonetheless (I don't remember seeing Bloomberg TV listed among the supporters of the bill on the Judiciary Committee website, which might have had something to do with it). http://www.bloomberg.com/video/83688294-reddit-com-opposition-to-stop-online-piracy-act.html

18. http://www.nytimes.com/2012/01/02/business/media/the-danger-of-an-attack-on-piracy-online.html?_r=4&pagewanted=all

Virtually every traditional media company in the United States loudly and enthusiastically supported SOPA, but that doesn't mean it's good for the rest of us. The open consumer Web has been a motor of American innovation and the attempt to curtail some of its excesses could throw sand in the works of a big machine on which we have all come to rely.

With the mainstream media—especially US television news outlets—shirking its duty to inform the public, the task of teaching people about SOPA and PIPA was basically left to the Internet.[19]

Lies, Damned Lies, and the Entertainment Industry

So even though Congress wasn't in session, I was spending my time in paradise on my laptop rather than with my girlfriend. Preparing for my testimony was even more nerveracking than that TED talk. As the day of my testimony drew closer, I researched as much as I could, calling friends who'd actually testified before Congress, watching ace testimonies on YouTube, and drafting my arguments. Meanwhile, the Internet public was busy doing such a tremendous job spreading the word about SOPA and PIPA that things

---

19. A Media Matters study found that "while U.S. television news outlets have largely ignored the controversial Stop Online Piracy Act during their evening news and opinion programming, they have covered repeatedly and at-length Tim Tebow, Casey Anthony, Kim Kardashian's divorce, the British Royal Family, and Alec Baldwin being kicked off an airplane." http://mediamatters.org/blog/2012/01/13/study-sopa-coverage-no-match-for-kim-kardashian/186175

really started falling apart for those bills that weekend. A new e-mail popped up in my in-box from a producer at MSNBC who wanted me to stop by *Up with Chris Hayes*[20] for a friendly chat with an executive from NBC as soon as I got back to New York. I jumped on it. The executive may have had the home field advantage, but I had millions of Americans at my back.

The following Saturday night, with my House Oversight Committee hearing just a few days away, Darrell Issa issued a press release at 1:00 a.m.[21] announcing the postponement of the hearing. Some of SOPA's supporters in the House were finally getting the message. On top of that, the White House was about to make a statement in response to petitions from citizens in opposition to these bills: "We will not support legislation that reduces freedom of expression, increases cybersecurity risk, or undermines the dynamic, innovative global Internet."[22] Zing. I wasn't going back to Washington after all.[23]

But our work was far from over. That Sunday, refreshed but without a tan, I showed up for my appearance on MSNBC. I figured our efforts must have really upset the guys in the executive lounge, because my counterpart turned out to be

---

20. http://upwithchrishayes.msnbc.com/_news/2012/01/15/10161056 -debating-sopa

21. I won't tell you what I was probably doing at that time, but I will say that I was enjoying my last night of vacation.

22. https://petitions.whitehouse.gov/response/combating-online-piracy -while-protecting-open-and-innovative-internet

23. Sorry, Sabriya!!!

Rick Cotton, executive vice president and general counsel of NBCUniversal. Considering the momentum we were gathering, he must not have had a very good weekend.

Before the interview, I was in the MSNBC greenroom with Jack Abramoff, lamenting the deleterious effects that lobbying was having on politics. Agreeing with Jack Abramoff is a weird feeling, but he told me he had never seen anything like this before—the entertainment industry almost always gets its way. There was significantly less banter between Mr. Cotton and me once he entered.

Everyone got a quick dose of makeup, and we were escorted to our assigned seats on the stage. No one touched the breakfast foods on the table. Pro tip: I've learned from multiple TV appearances now that the food on the table is in fact edible. As one who hates wasting food, I'll usually nosh off-camera and then obsessively make sure there's nothing stuck in my teeth before the camera blinks red again. That morning, however, I left the muffins alone. Too nervous. I'd prepared for a lot of things, but I hadn't prepared for Richard Cotton to come out with a full arsenal of frenzied malarkey.[24]

There was no discussion—just Cotton's barrage of misleading talking points and interruptions. I was frustrated. I'd done live television before—the goal is to say as much as you can in as few words as possible and look confident doing it—but I'd never done live television in this format before.

Cotton opened by stressing a point that the entertain-

---

24. http://www.techdirt.com/articles/20120116/01350817412/lies-nbcuniversals-rick-cotton-about-sopapipa.shtml

ment industry had been repeating from the start: "This leg-islation would not affect a single site in the United States." I've already pointed out that American companies, includ-ing payment processors and advertising networks, would have had to stop doing business with certain websites sim-ply because a private company had filed a notice of infringe-ment. Furthermore, Steve and I could not have started reddit if we had been liable for every piece of user-generated con-tent on the site, nor could any website with user-generated content have begun or survived.

Even more frustrating was that this lawyer was effectively telling an entrepreneur, "I know your own company better than you do." What I should have said was this: "Yes, actu-ally, American companies—like mine—would be affected. You can tell from the first few pages of the bill alone, the definitions section, that the writer lacked the technologi-cal understanding to even correctly distinguish foreign from domestic websites: American companies with foreign domain names are called 'foreign Internet sites.' I'm here this morning not only because *my* American company would be affected but also because countless more American com-panies would be affected. Companies that exist today may never exist tomorrow because of these bills."

Unfortunately, that's not what I said. What actually fell out of my mouth was something more like:

"What troubles me is that...for instance...the anticir-cumvention policies would lump reddit, or really any..."

Ugh. Fail. I go on to discuss the nuances of a provision of the bills that First Amendment expert Marvin Ammori warns could be interpreted to require any website that contains user-generated content (from reddit to a personal blog that allows comments) to police every single piece of content for any information about circumvention information (such as where to illegally download the latest *Fast & Furious* sequel). If the site didn't comply, it would risk legal action.[25] It's simply unfeasible to police an entire website of user-generated content on which there could be hundreds, or thousands, or tens of thousands (you get the point) of new entries every minute. But that was way too many words for a Sunday morning talk show.

Cotton interrupted me.

"That is simply wrong!" he exclaimed.

I continued, trying to remain calm. Inside, I'm flipping out. Fortunately, the camera wasn't on me, because the veins in my forehead undoubtedly started to bulge.

While I was stumbling, Cotton was deftly tweaking his message. "This legislation is devoted exclusively to foreign sites."

See what he did there? It may be *devoted exclusively* to foreign sites, but if it happens to wipe out domestic sites, so it goes—it's still *devoted exclusively* to foreign sites, and the domestic sites are collateral damage. Suddenly Laurence Tribe's "blunderbuss" metaphor really hits home: the barrel of these bills is pointed abroad, but domestic sites and Internet users are in the line of fire. And that simply will not do.

I got my chance for redemption on the morning of the

---

25. http://ammori.org/2011/12/31/sopapipa-copyright-bills-also-target -domestic-sites/

protests, with Soledad O'Brien on CNN.[26] This time, I made sure to emphasize simply and unequivocally how bad these bills would be for our freedom to connect. Did I mention that the tech industry was one of the healthiest sectors of the US economy, a source of optimism and innovation even in the middle of a recession? "If [SOPA and PIPA] had existed," I told Soledad, "Steve Huffman and I could have never started reddit. It's frustrating to see legislation that was written by lobbyists and not technologists perhaps become law." And then I went for the jugular, with a sound bite crafted in response to scores of great online comments about my MSNBC interview:

> I just wish we had been called to the table when this legislation was written....It's just so frustrating because we look at Congress and we can't see them do anything that's important. They can't solve the problems of unemployment, they can't solve the problems of the deficit. Yet as soon as a lobbyist shows up with ninety-four million dollars, Democrats and Republicans line up to co-sponsor it. Something is wrong.[27]

And we had a solution.

---

26. http://www.mediaite.com/tv/soledad-obrien-grills-reddit-founder-on-the-sites-sopa-inspired-shut-down/

27. Not only did software engineer Joel Spolsky insist I wear a red tie for my day of interviews and protest, he also suggested this line, which became the sound bite of the day for an audience that may not have understood everything about the technology but could relate to dysfunctional politics funded by lobbying money.

Geeks in the Streets

That same day, NY Tech Meetup, a group of more than thirty thousand New York City–based technologists, organized an emergency meeting to protest the bills at the offices of the New York senators. After I left CNN, I raced across midtown to do what I could to help.

I made it to the protest just as it was setting up. Thousands of New Yorkers showed up on a surprisingly sunny winter afternoon in midtown (where nerds fear to tread—so you know this was important). We were protesting in front of the offices of Senators Gillibrand and Schumer, both of whom supported the Senate bill, PIPA, which was reeling but still up for discussion.

The protesters were angry but polite, their signs clever and without spelling or grammatical errors. In most cases the protesters were even reasonably well dressed—they all looked like people you'd enjoy sitting next to on the subway. Entire offices in the New York tech community had emptied out to come here. Most people would rather have been back in the office inventing the future, but today that future was threatened.

Swarms of reporters gathered around the small stage and modest audio setup. One sign said it all—it also happened to become the iconic image from the protest: IT'S NO LONGER OK TO *NOT* KNOW HOW THE INTERNET WORKS.[28]

The person holding it wasn't a fresh-faced geeky male in a

---

28. http://www.flickr.com/photos/photo_td/6746861781/

hoodie, either. It was a middle-aged woman wearing a stern look and carrying an even sterner message for her lawmakers.

There were speakers (including me), but there was no one leader—ours was a leader*ful* movement. Not unlike the net itself.

Speaking in front of an audience of a few thousand members of the New York tech community, I used the opportunity to emphasize the issue that a country in recession cares most about—jobs. When I was called to the stage, the microphone was a good foot too short for me, so I awkwardly stood half on the platform and half off. Good enough. As long as they saw me only from the waist up, they'd never know how weird I looked standing there.

"We're here because we're fighting against the wholesale—wholesale—destruction of one of the healthiest parts of America's economy," I said.

This was the same way I had introduced myself to congressional representatives when I visited the Hill in November. It worked because it was true—we'd gotten to live the American dream thanks to an open Internet, and these bills would've made that impossible for us and all the other entrepreneurs you've been reading about who rely upon the Internet to help themselves.

"Can I get a show of hands—how many of you are working at companies that are hiring?"

As a founder, investor, and adviser, I knew this was the right question to ask the Internet audience. Nearly every hand went up.

"Can the journalists get a look here? Look at all the

companies, America, that are looking to hire Americans right now."

And on it went. After that talk I dashed off to the closest café that had wireless Internet access and Skyped into another interview. There was a last-minute CNBC interview I had to phone in on a mobile phone—I still regret not having a landline for that one. By the time I caught my breath I was wrapping up an interview on Fox Business and figuring out a dinner reservation for me and my girlfriend so I could start to make up for the vacation snafu. The day had gone rather well, I thought.[29] It wasn't until the next day, though, that I realized the magnitude of what we'd all done.

It was unprecedented. Within a day, thirteen senators had switched sides—five of whom had been co-sponsors of the bill: Blunt, Boozman, Cardin, Hatch, and Rubio. And after a day of protest, phone calls, and petitions, the American people triumphed over tens of millions of lobbying dollars.

Turns out the Supreme Court, in its 1997 "town crier" decision (where the Internet enables anyone to be a "town crier," only with far more impact), wasn't far off, as Yochai Benkler says: "Not everyone is a pamphleteer, but…what you see is a complex relationship between NGOs and commercial organizations; between VCs and activists; between traditional media and online media; between political media left and right; and tech media; all weaving together a model of actually looking,

---

29. I even got a nice nod from *The New Yorker*, which took a moment to point out my white-shirt-red-tie combo—brilliantly suggested by my friend and fellow tech CEO Joel Spolsky. I borrowed the tie from my dad.

learning, mobilizing for action, and blocking. This, ideally, is the shape of the networked public sphere."[30]

This was a leaderful movement, full of people who found ways to help, whether it was as simple as changing their profile photos, calling their senators, and brainstorming ideas for boycotts and protests or writing the code that would parse the fund-raising data and show just how much Hollywood had paid each senator and representative.

We had made a connection with our fellow Americans, who got involved at every level. We had formed a decentralized but powerful lobbying group—the American people.

But would it make a difference?

Internet FTW

Thanks to the online and off-line protests, by January 19, some of SOPA's and PIPA's most prominent backers were publicly running from the bills, leaving only fifty-five supporters and co-sponsors (with 205 opposed) once everyone caught their breath.[31] Not only was my House panel canceled because of the momentum swing, SOPA's chief sponsor, Representative Lamar Smith (R-Texas), announced that the bill was being recalled in the House.

On the same day that SOPA was recalled in the House, Senate majority leader Harry Reid (D-Nevada) announced

---

30. http://www.youtube.com/watch?feature=player_embedded&v=LNP9f8geCWA

31. http://projects.propublica.org/sopa/

that the Senate was postponing the vote on PIPA. I'd like to translate his statement (my translations in *italics*):[32]

"I admire the work that Chairman Leahy has put into this bill."

Pat got a cameo in The Dark Knight! *I thought for sure this was my ticket for at least a speaking role in the next* Transformers, *but now I'll be lucky to be an extra in an Adam Sandler film.*

"I encourage him to continue engaging with all stakeholders to forge a balance between protecting Americans' intellectual property and maintaining openness and innovation on the Internet."

Apparently millions of Americans use the Internet and love freedom. Perhaps we should consult people outside of the entertainment industry the next time we write a law about the Internet. Maybe invite some people who understand how it works, too.

"We made good progress through the discussions we've held in recent days, and I am optimistic that we can reach a compromise in the coming weeks."

We've never seen anything like this before. Seriously. Dollars always won in Washington until millions of citizens making phone calls, writing e-mails, drawing up petitions, and organizing protests ruined everything. I'm going to pretend like I'm optimistic about compromise to try to save face, but really, the American people have spoken loud and clear.

---

32. http://democrats.senate.gov/2012/01/20/reid-statement-on
-intellectual-property-bill/

Fatality; Internet freedom wins.[33]

Representative Zoe Lofgren (D-CA) put it best: "This bill went from being inevitable to unthinkable thanks to the American people."[34]

January 18, 2012, was a watershed moment for the Internet. We had done something Congress had never seen before[35]—we triumphed over millions of lobbying dollars and decades of "relationship building" between the entertainment industry and Congress. And no one person or group organized it. You've heard my story, but it was by no means the only one, let alone the most important—hardly. There were millions of stories in the fight to defeat these awful bills. Disparate people from all over came together, contributed in whatever ways they could, and we accomplished something far greater than any one of us could have accomplished individually. It's fitting that the preservation of the Internet would be accomplished in a manner so similar to the way the network itself proliferated. There was no top-down plan for the World Wide Web; it just started growing organically as people contributed ideas and built websites. The Internet is simultaneously the world's biggest library and a stage. It was a tragedy of civilization when the Library of Alexandria burned, but in truth, it would infinitely be worse if that should happen to the World Wide Web.

---

33. This is to be read in the Mortal Kombat voice.

34. Representative Lofgren said this during the DC screening of our documentary, *Silicon Prairie: America's New Internet Economy*.

35. http://arstechnica.com/tech-policy/2013/01/republican-staffer-fired-for-copyright-memo-talks-to-ars/

Not only do we never want the Internet destroyed, we must outline just how we want to expand access to it. There was so much momentum generated by the debate about SOPA and PIPA—and eventually ACTA (Anti-Counterfeiting Trade Agreement), which shortly thereafter was thwarted in Europe—that we're now looking to draft legislation that secures online rights just as other legislation protects rights off-line. To that end, a number of us (including some awesome open Internet champions, such as Josh Levy, Elizabeth Stark, Seth Bannon, Tiffiniy Cheng, Holmes Wilson, and Ben Huh) created the Declaration of Internet Freedom, which we published on July 4, 2012, and which has since been translated into more than sixty-five languages and signed by hundreds of corporations and individuals (including US senators and representatives). Deliberately basic, the declaration is meant to be a fundamental statement of

Internet philosophy that any elected official would agree to because they know their constituents wouldn't have it any other way. Here it is:

> We support transparent and participatory processes for making Internet policy and the establishment of five basic principles:
>
> **Expression:** Don't censor the Internet.
>
> **Access:** Promote universal access to fast and affordable networks.
>
> **Openness:** Keep the Internet an open network where everyone is free to connect, communicate, write, read, watch, speak, listen, learn, create, and innovate.
>
> **Innovation:** Protect the freedom to innovate and create without permission. Don't block new technologies and don't punish innovators for their users' actions.
>
> **Privacy:** Protect privacy and defend everyone's ability to control how their data and devices are used.
>
> http://www.internetdeclaration.org/freedom

As signatures continue to climb, we've also formed the Internet Defense League, a project begun by the nonprofit organization Fight for the Future, which allows anyone with a web presence (not just a website with millions of visitors but even a Twitter account with a few followers) to sign up and be notified the next time we need to take collective action to save the Internet. We hope it won't happen again soon, or ever, but just in case, the nonprofit has readied a "Cat-Signal" that will call everyone to action. Not unlike a Bat-Signal (but we certainly don't want any copyright lawyers calling us!) for the open Internet, it's a way to sign up to be a Batman or Batwoman for your own digital Gotham. And you needn't be a billionaire with anger management issues—you just need Internet access. Whether you have an online community of a dozen Twitter followers or a website that's read by millions, you have a parcel of the Internet you want to protect. The SOPA and PIPA protests showed millions of people just how much power they had when using this great platform to connect and do something formerly unthinkable; should we need to use it again, we'll be ready.

It's Up to Us to Keep the Internet Free (and Keep This Book Relevant)

Fortunately, we've got a lot of momentum on our side. Ever since January 18, 2012, Congress has been terrified of getting "SOPA'd"[36] again; and as we press forward the positive agenda to proactively support and promote Internet freedom, it's important to never lose sight of the fact that opponents will continue to find ways to curtail our online rights. That's why organizations like Fight for the Future are so important. But they can only do so much and are ultimately only as effective as their communities. The Internet public will continue to be the most valuable component of innovation, but only if we continue to enjoy the same online freedoms that we enjoy off-line. It's not only because of sheer numbers—though it does matter—it's also because of creativity. In aggregate, millions of disparate, independent people can perform phenomenal works of collaboration never possible before the connected web. The vast network of open-source projects that made nearly all the aforementioned stories possible is the result of countless hours of work from all over the world, all for a purpose not explicitly defined.

The movement for Internet freedom is similarly structured. Furthermore, all political movements will begin to show a similar DNA, if they're not already. To wit, the Tea Party and the Occupy movement have little in common when it comes to political agendas, but their networks are incredibly

---

36. http://www.politico.com/news/stories/0312/73802.html

widely distributed and their hierarchies virtually nonexistent. Both groups are distributed across the country and both believe their government doesn't represent them—the people. They disagree on what to do about that, but it's rather striking that their common bond is rooted in making the government more accountable to its citizens, something we really saw for the first time at the national level during the SOPA and PIPA discussions. It also shouldn't come as a surprise that the Internet freedom movement found support in both camps.[37] The future of US politics in a connected world is still being written.

These days, presidential debates are being discussed in real time online, memes are created within seconds (think "horses and bayonets" from the third 2012 presidential debate), and we're learning about Newark mayor Cory Booker's post-Sandy cleanup effort from his personal Twitter account.[38] Politicians work for us, and we have the technology to see their work as it's happening, just as we can see that delicious *stroopwafel* someone photographed with their smartphone. Demand for access to government data is waxing, but we don't have nearly enough people capable of analyzing it and using it to help us help ourselves do everything better—whether it's getting status updates on the BxM10

---

37. http://occupywallstreet.net/story/statement-against-sopa and http://www.redstate.com/erick/2011/12/22/stopping-sopa/

38. During a rather difficult time for us in the New York region, Mayor Booker's humorous tweets became a thing of legend. In response to a tweet from an Irishman complaining about a pothole, he wrote, "Sir, it looks like you live in Dublin, Ireland. I've got 99 problems & your ditch ain't one." https://twitter.com/CoryBooker/statuses/265520644991619073?tw_i=265520644991619073

bus or organizing a Crowdtilt project to finally get that pothole fixed.

More and more people are turning to one another on the
Internet to solve real problems—not as a replacement for government but as a supplement that responds in real time and
builds community as it helps others. Shortly after Hurricane
Sandy devastated the greater New York and New Jersey area,
the Occupy Sandy relief effort was launched to organize
hundreds if not thousands of volunteers to rebuild communities and get assistance to those who needed it most. There
was no memo. No one stopped to ask for approval to help.
They just did it.

We'll do everything we can to protect the open Internet,
so we can live to see the day when all of us are on the playing field with the same access to online resources and the
ability to live life to its fullest. I have no idea what tomorrow will bring. But the more chances we take on people with
small ideas, the better off our world will be. In the meantime, call your politicians to find out how much they're
doing for Internet freedom. They work for us, after all. And
like any good boss, you should check up on your employees.
There's no excuse for us not to know how things are going,
because if this technology lets us see photos of what Kim
Kardashian had for brunch, it absolutely should let us have
real-time access to what our government is doing with our
tax dollars and trust.

CHAPTER NINE

Dear Graduating
Class of 2025

Good news, everyone!

Professor Hubert J. Farnsworth

The problem with the future is that none of it's guaranteed.

I debated how best to illustrate my vision for 2025, but everything felt a bit forced until my brilliant editor suggested framing it as a commencement speech for someone just finishing college in 2025. Now, it feels rather presumptuous to expect to be speaking at a college graduation, but I went along with it—after giving you nine chapters of optimism, I thought it might be important to give you a grim look at what could happen if we do nothing over the next decade or so.

Although it is only mid-May, the summer heat is suffocating. Alexis Ohanian lumbers over to the lectern, wearing the drab gray smock considered fashionable in this era of stifled creativity. He wipes the sweat from his brow, clears his throat, and speaks.

Dear Graduating Class of 2025: I owe you an apology. We screwed up the Internet, one of the world's greatest innovations, and I'm truly sorry. Also, I'm really sorry about the climate change. Perspective is everything, though. I mean, look at how much more we appreciate the parts of the Eastern Seaboard that aren't underwater now. Besides, who really liked polar bears, anyway?

As for the Internet, we had a chance, with all the momentum we gained from pummeling SOPA and PIPA back in 2012, to educate our politicians about how important Internet freedom is to every single one of their constituents. Every member of the House and Senate represented a digital district—it wasn't a red or blue issue, but something that even the most divisive districts could agree on. Despite what you may've heard or read, it wasn't just Silicon Valley that cared about this; *it was all of America.*

I hope you've read in your history books about Silicon Valley and all the burgeoning startup communities around the country at that time. We were one of the few sectors hiring back then; in fact, we couldn't hire enough. Some of your parents might have even been part of that scene. Geez... hmm... this probably isn't what you need to hear right now, given the bleak state of the economy you're graduating into. Back in the day, software was eating the world, creating jobs and innovation, until we put protecting Mickey Mouse on a higher pedestal than protecting the free market. At least we've got that new 3-D version of *Fast & Furious: Part XII*. Seriously, they're still trying to make 3-D a thing?

Anyhow, we were on the verge of major innovations across multiple industries. For one thing, your educational experience might have been very different if you had had access to a free Internet, no matter where or even whether you went to college. Imagine being able to take free classes from the world's best instructors any time you wanted. That was happening. Nonprofits and for-profits alike were all engineering better ways for anyone with an Internet connection to get an education. It looked like universal Internet access for all Americans was becoming a priority for our politicians. I used to be able to look a person in the eye and say if she wanted to learn to become a programmer and build the next reddit, she or he could go online right now and get started. It was the same way Steve Huffman had learned much of what he used to build reddit and hipmunk. There were no gatekeepers.

But I can't say that today. To make matters worse, your tuition payments rose to levels that have left most of you deeply in debt. Keep that in mind as you toss those mortarboards in the air. Or don't—actually, now that I think about it, I don't think you're allowed to do that.

But even if meaningful employment isn't on the horizon for many or even most of you, don't worry! One of the perks of unemployment is all the free time you'll have to surf the GoogleVerizonComcastNet©™ from your parents' basement. There was a time when we had competition and a flat

Internet, where all links were created equal. We all thought of it as a sort of public utility back then—so quaint. Today, of course, the only search engine most of us can afford to use always gives us erection pill ads as the first page of results.

In case you find yourselves wondering what life was like back then, you can always fire up Gmail. Google hasn't had to update it in nearly a decade because there's no reason to— no startup can compete with them because they just block that competitor's website or bury them in litigation.

Now, I'm seeing some funny looks out there in the audience. Yes, it's true that bright young people like you used to build things all the time, and some of those projects turned into entrepreneurial endeavors—remarkable things that made the world suck less.

But I guess I'm really showing my age.

Just this morning I found a polite note in my Dropbox from the federal agent who investigated a "suspicious" photo I'd privately stored there from a family vacation. I'd done nothing wrong, of course, but he was just letting me know they had run a quick search. At least he left a note, right? Believe it or not, there was a time when we truly believed our digital storage was as private as our physical storage. Want to enter my home? Sure, get a warrant—same goes for my Dropbox. Those were the days. . . .

These days, of course, the government doesn't need any due process to read our e-mail or search any of those formerly private messaging services, because they decided that the Fourth Amendment applies only to physical mail. Hey, remember when we used to have post offices and mailboxes and letters? No? Ask your parents.

Seriously, people used to think that digital privacy was just as important as physical privacy. That concept might seem antiquated to you all now, but when I was your age, if someone was illegally opening your mail, it was customary to punch them in the throat.

I know it's not polite to bring this up, but a little while after January 18, 2012, it seemed like our government would have a new level of accountability. Congress had abysmal approval ratings back then—worse than colonoscopies[1]—yet the Internet public realized that the connected web could give them leverage over even the richest and most entrenched lobbying groups. We had our congressional representatives and senators on speed dial. We would call them to check up on things and correct them when they did something bad— just as a good boss should. We paid their salaries, we hired and fired them—why shouldn't we know what they're up to? Social media, which gave us unprecedented access into the mundane lives of strangers, made us feel entitled to know what our elected officials were doing and helped us to hold them accountable. It even looked like we were going to develop better politicians in the process, as their attention became more focused on their voters than on the biggest donors to their campaigns. That was silly and naive of us.

Back when I finished my first book, *Without Their Permission*, I really thought we were going to make the right decisions, too. The open Internet, as a platform, used to embody

---

1. Seriously. Colonoscopies save lives. If you're more than fifty years old you should absolutely talk to your doctor about this lifesaving cancer screening test. http://www.nytimes.com/2012/02/23/health/colonoscopy-prevents-cancer -deaths-study-finds.html?pagewanted=all

so many of the highest ideals of this country. Our Internet was filled with the true spirit of innovation, entrepreneurship, helping yourself as well as others, and the freedom to connect whenever you want—as well as the right to privacy when you don't. We could have been real role models for the world. Our bad, guys.

Well, now I've got a flight back to Shanghai to catch. It's a shame I had to move my company there, but the level and quantity of science, engineering, technology, and math talent over there made it an easy business decision. It's sad because of how much I loved not only this country but also the freedom to innovate and tinker, which encouraged so many of us back then.

I'm truly sorry. We had a great opportunity, but we failed, and now it's you all, our future, who are left with the consequences. The irony isn't lost on me—we all let it happen without your permission.

Yikes. That would have been a terrible way to end this book. Let me try again.

Here's how we could do better....

Not only did we successfully defend the open Internet, we pushed for reforms that promoted innovation and equal access. After all, the American public had already spoken loud and clear about their support for Internet freedom. My friend Erik Martin and I saw it firsthand on the Internet 2012 Bus Tour. It really hit home early one morning in rural Richmond, Missouri, as we all feasted on breakfast courtesy of farmer Tom Parker and his family. Tom's industry is one of the oldest in America—agriculture—and he confessed to checking his e-mail only three times a week. For me, a geek in Brooklyn, checking only three times in an hour seems low, but the Internet economy has already drastically changed the Parker family farm. More than 90 percent of Tom's customers now come to him through the Internet, thanks to a Kansas City–based startup called AgLocal. It may have been the delicious second helping of eggs I'd just eaten, but it was there on that farm, with cows mooing in the background, that I realized just what an impact the Internet was having. Tom Parker gets it: "Putting family farms on a level playing field can only happen because the cost of sharing a story on the Internet is nothing."[2] We need to make sure his elected representatives get it, too.

That's why we did the bus tour, and why our friends at NimbleBot filmed a documentary about the journey, *Silicon Prairie: America's New Internet Economy*, which inspired others around the world to do the same for their own local Internet economies. We screened our film to a packed room at the Newseum in Washington, DC. The four sitting US representatives (two Republicans and two Democrats) in attendance celebrated the film and what it stood for. It stood, of course, for progress. Whether we worry about big government or big business, let's not allow either one of them to ruin one of mankind's greatest innovations.

We'll continue to triumph over misinformation, despite

---

2. http://www.adweek.com/internet-2012/internet-powering-local-food
-movement-144390

the best efforts of a few to stifle the freedom of the many. The onus is on all of us to educate each and every one of our elected officials. Should governments ever make the tragic decision that intellectual property is actual property and enforce strict penalties for blurring the distinction, most forms of online speech would become violations of IP law. Copying a digital file (such as a picture of a car) is not theft, because the original picture is still entirely intact; you just have two of them now. Stealing a car is theft, because the original car is not in the place it was before. Please refer, people, to this handy chart:

Our Internet-enabled computing devices are essentially copy machines that make all the ingenuity we see online possible. There is no viable technological alternative, because it's the very nature of the platform. It's the freedom inherent in the open Internet that has enabled and empowered Steve and me, Charles Best, Debby Guardino, Zach Anner, Zach Weinersmith, Lester Chambers, and countless others around the world. Less than ten years earlier, none of their achievements would have been possible. Imagine what just a decade more of Internet freedom will do.

That's how fast innovation moves online—not just for startups, but also, as I've shown, in the fields of art, activism, philanthropy, and politics. Every industry is getting swallowed up as code eats the world, and the result is a free and flat network. That's why bridging the digital divide is so important—it's part access and part education, and it's all vital both to the health of our nations and to our Internet. A quality Internet connection is a public utility that should be accessible to all people, regardless of how much money they have and where they live. If we believe every American has a right to electricity, why would we withhold humanity's greatest omnidirectional flow of information?

The Internet (called ARPANET back in its infancy) was born in America with a connection between two computers, one at UCLA and the other in Menlo Park, California. Yet today, "nineteen million Americans, many in rural areas... can't get access to a high-speed connection at any price, it's just not there. And for a third of all Americans...it's just too expensive."[3] That's research from Susan Crawford, law professor and technology expert, who has done tremendous

---

3. http://vimeo.com/59236702

work bringing this reality to light and letting us know that we should all take action to give Americans the access they deserve. Children in twenty-first-century America shouldn't have to go to McDonald's to do their homework, yet that's what they do.[4] How else can we, the country that currently leads the world in the Internet industry (and there aren't many industries we still dominate globally), continue to keep our competitive edge?

"We hold these truths to be self-evident, that all men are created equal." Those are the words of Thomas Jefferson with which I began chapter 2. Equality is an ideal we still strive for, but it is truly encapsulated in the technology of the World Wide Web. It's fitting that those words were referenced in Dr. Martin Luther King's "I Have a Dream" speech, which is itself a glorious remix, sampling the Bible, the Gettysburg Address, "My Country, 'Tis of Thee," and even Shakespeare. It's arguably the most famous speech of twentieth-century American history—but it's also still under copyright, so you can't watch it unless someone pays for it.

Originally, the length of copyright in the United States was fourteen years. This is far beyond what our Founding Fathers outlined. Thanks to lobbying by the entertainment industry—in the decades before we had a connected Internet public to combat such awful legislation—copyright now extends for the life of the author plus at least seventy years.[5] Jefferson even proposed putting an explicit limit on

---

4. http://online.wsj.com/article/SB10001424127887324731304578189794161056954.html

5. This may come as shocking news, but the Sonny Bono Copyright Term Extension Act of 1998 did just that.

copyright length into the Bill of Rights.[6] T.J. recognized, even back then, how important it was to keep information as free as possible. If his amendment had made it into the final draft, then we could all freely watch Dr. King's historic speech whenever we wanted. Instead, we still fight, not just for reasonable copyright reform but also to nurture great ideas before they're bullied out of existence.

This entire book was made possible thanks to a free Internet. The first part was my own story of startup success, but my story is just one of many. I could very likely be writing a chapter in my next book (should I be so lucky) about you.[7] It won't be easy; you'll need to develop your skills, work hard, and get a good dose of luck, but a computer, an Internet connection, and time are the only raw materials required.

The sad reality is that there are still too many people who don't have access to the Internet, and if they do, they don't have the skills to master it. This book cannot provide an Internet connection for you (believe me, if it could, it would), so I wrote the second part because I want you to save your money and not bother getting an MBA. This book is way cheaper.[8] Beyond that, there are opportunities to learn from communities both online and off-line. We humans have been making connections for the purpose of learning and

---

6. Here's what he proposed as article 9: "Monopolies may be allowed to persons for their own productions in literature and their own inventions in the arts for a term not exceeding ___ years but for no longer term and no other purpose." http://www.founding.com/founders_library/pageID.2184/default.asp

7. In fact, if you go on to do great things after reading this book, please e-mail me so I can take all the credit for it.

8. If you paid more than five figures for this book, immediately seek a refund.

sharing information since the beginning of time. Whether you're learning how to build your first Android application or sharing your thoughts about Twilight Sparkle,[9] the Internet has made that a whole lot more efficient. Every day I encounter people who are using the Internet to pursue their dreams or to enrich their lives, but we need more of them.

By the way, being entrepreneurial is not limited to entrepreneurs. The last part of this book is a testament to that. Charles Best, Debby Guardino, Zach Anner, Zach Weinersmith, Lester Chambers, and countless participants in the fight against SOPA and PIPA wouldn't necessarily be thought of as traditional entrepreneurs, but in spirit, they are undoubtedly entrepreneurial. They've found success because they could use this great equalizer—the open Internet—to spread their ideas, find their audiences, and ultimately surmount traditional barriers.

The open Internet is not a magic wand, but as a technology it has the potential to do tremendous things—to allow awesome people to reach their full potential. It is ultimately incumbent upon us, as builders and users of this platform, to see that it lives up to its own full potential. As we look, wide-eyed, into the future, let's remember that the baggage of our society comes with us online. While the Internet as a technology is flat, as long as all links are equal, the world we live in is still full of inequality. Most of my now-lionized peers, the founders of the Internet's original startups, are straight white young men. But as it turns out, the world is not full of only young straight white guys—in fact, far from it. What excites me so much about this technology is how it

---

9. My Little Pony protagonist. If you didn't know, now you do.

democratizes knowledge as well as distribution. But the system lives up to its full potential only if all of us have access and the skills to make the most out of it.

In sum, it's not enough to just go forth and create without asking anyone's permission, or to help others who are trying to do the same. Like the Internet itself, we are greater than just the sum of our parts. We're not yet taking full advantage of all our parts, but we get closer every day, thanks to all the individuals and organizations striving toward it. Think of all the genius the world has missed out on simply because otherwise awesome people got bad "life lottery" tickets. It motivates me and many more to work toward building an open Internet, if for no other reason than it's going to mean better stuff—better businesses and better nonprofits, better artists and better activists, and, yes, even better politicians. It's going to enable awesome people to actually be awesome in a way that they couldn't have been before.

Remember, this is just the beginning. Everything I've written about has happened only in the last decade, which is but a moment given the speed of innovation online. Imagine what this next decade will bring. Every child who grows up with an Internet connection and the skills to make the most of it is yet another potential founder, or artist, or activist, or philanthropist, or…I don't know, that's just it: I can look her in the eyes and tell her that she doesn't need to ask anyone's permission to go learn about the printing press, or start publishing her photography, or rally her community to fix a dilapidated playground, or begin working on the next big thing. No, none of these things are going to be easy, but

I'm certainly not going to be the one to tell her she can't do them.

Let me put it this way: if the Industrial Revolution changed the world, the current revolution, powered by software and the Internet, is destined to do the same, but far more democratically. Instead of opening a factory, you need only open your laptop.

I hope you're convinced. And more important, I trust you'll do something good with that conviction. Spread the word, give this book to someone who needs to read it, put your politicians on notice, and make things people love.

Start.

Please.

What are you waiting for? Someone's permission?

Acknowledgments

I had no idea what I was getting myself into in terms of writing a book, and I'm grateful to everyone who helped along the way.

My editor, Rick Wolff, took a chance on a serial entrepreneur but first-time author and even indulged my fondness for waffles on more than one occasion. (There are no Waffle Houses in New York City, so we go to IHOP.) I hope the fate of this book makes you look really prescient. I also want to thank Rick's brilliant team at Business Plus, including Meredith Haggerty, Amanda Pritzker, Carolyn Kurek, Barbara Clark, and Liz Connor (what a cool book cover!).

The person who first said, "Yeah, you should write a book," was Erin Malone, my agent. What she doesn't know is that after meeting her, I canceled all my other meetings with prospective agents. Thanks, Erin.

My girlfriend, Sabriya Stukes, put up with the late nights of writing, frantic last-minute backups, and has generally put up with someone who works as much as I do. Now that my book is done, I'm going to take you on a nice vacation—someplace with no Internet!

Justin Keenan helped make everything I wrote awesome

before I even sent it to Rick. His edits and suggestions were always delivered with humor I didn't know was capable via Microsoft Word's Track Changes. I've yet to meet him in person; the Internet rocks.

Kathrina Manalac, Christina Xu, and Joe Alger all make my life (and thus this book) possible.

I'm a lucky guy for having so many acclaimed writers for friends, to whom I've looked both in admiration as well as for advice. Thank you, Jenny 8. Lee, Tim Wu, Clay Shirky, Drew Curtis, Eddie Huang, and Shama Kabani.

Steve Huffman, because if we hadn't been living across the hall from each other our first year at the University of Virginia, I'd probably be an immigration lawyer. Without you, there'd be no book to write. This book doesn't do your talents justice, so please write one of your own and let me blurb it.

Dr. Chris Slowe and Kristen Sakillaris, you two are adorable together, but still not as adorable as my favorite un-god-daughter. Chris, Steve and I couldn't have moved into a better apartment after Y Combinator. How fortuitous. Grateful to call you both friends.

Thanks to Paul Graham, Jessica Livingston, Trevor Blackwell, and Robert Morris of Y Combinator for taking a chance on two fresh-faced UVA graduates, thus altering the course of our lives. In fact, my entire Y Combinator family is awesome. You all rock.

I am grateful to all my book subjects for taking the time to open up about their lives and ambitions. Charles Best, Debby Guardino, Lester and Dylan Chambers, Zach Anner, and Zach Weinersmith—you all inspire me. (Mr. Weinersmith much less so than the rest of you.) Thank you for being some of the best examples of what an open Internet can do.

Erik Martin, you sly dog. I know you remember what a big deal it was when the first talkies appeared, so your perspective on the Internet's potential is especially valuable. The Internet 2012 Bus Tour never would've happened without you, or if it had, it would've been demonstrably less fabulous. Thank you for your friendship and your beard. In fact, thanks to everyone who not only made that bus tour possible, but made it so grand.

For everyone who has fought and continues to fight for Internet freedom. I get more credit than I deserve. You all are the minutemen and -women making sure there's an open World Wide Web for our grandchildren; I just get to be a town crier. Tif Cheng, Holmes Wilson, Derek Slater, Mike Masnick, Michael Petricone, Laurent Crenshaw, Seamus Kraft, Ben Huh, Eli Pariser, Elizabeth Stark, Andrew Rasiej, Marvin Ammori, Craig Newmark, Josh Levy, Seth Bannon, Susan Crawford, and everyone at organizations like Fight for the Future, Engine Advocacy, Demand Progress, New York Tech Meetup, Electronic Frontier Foundation, Free Press, Public Knowledge, and all the countless others whose names I'll never know.

Writing a book while you're also running and investing in startups doesn't leave much free time, but I've got very understanding friends who forgave me for being even less responsive during my infamous "month of e-mail autoresponder." Thanks especially to S. I. Newhouse, Dr. Huu Nguyen, and Andy Pham. And thanks to my new family—my two sisters Amy and Hayley, and Charlotte—you all are so incredibly supportive of me even though I'm terrible about remembering to call home.

I had some life-changing professors during my four years at UVA—in particular Tom Bateman, Alon Confino, H. C. Erik Midelfort, Gordon Stewart, John Wheeler, and Mark White. Thank you for going above and beyond for the odd wahoo with green hair.

The crew who've been my best friends since elementary school: Paul Burt, Brian Femiano, Mike Scrivener, Adam Solomon, Asa Solomon, Jon Swyers, and Jacob Winthrop. You guys are in the book!

Stephen Colbert, we're not friends, but you got me through a really hard year. Your show, *The Colbert Report*, launched just a month or so after I got the news about my mom, and I can't even begin to tell you how much it did for me. Thank you for all the laughs, then and now.

I wrote most of my book during the 2012 NFL season, which had a really positive effect on my mood (and thus productivity) until the first round of the playoffs, so I must also acknowledge two 'Skins in particular: Alfred Morris and Robert Griffin III. Son or daughter, I'm naming him or her Robert Griffin Ohanian.

While I'm at it, nearly this entire book was written with either Jay-Z or Metallica (never both) playing in the background. One day we should all get brunch together. I'll tease Lars Ulrich about his quixotic crusade against MP3s; Hova will hassle me for buying up his shares in the Brooklyn Nets; we'll all laugh about the bizarre circumstances that brought us together.

I couldn't be here without all the haters. I want to acknowledge you, too. To everyone who ever put me down, discounted me, or even fired me: thank you. I've since taken down the "wall of negative reinforcement," but it's still in my head, motivating me to improve. I'm not done yet.

You really read this far, eh? That's pretty damn impressive. Thus, I'd like to also acknowledge you, dear reader, for you've absolutely gone above and beyond. Anyone can publish a book, but without readers it's just text. I hope you enjoyed it (go ahead and let me know, I'm @alexisohanian on Twitter).

Most important:

. Dad, thanks for naming me "Alexis," for demystifying entrepreneurship, and for showing me what it means to be a man. Mom, I miss you. I'll never match your compassion, kindness, or courage, but I'm going to keep trying.

Alexis Ohanian
Spring 2013

Index

About the Author

Alexis Ohanian became mayor of the Internet.
Forbes magazine, June 25, 2012

ALEXIS OHANIAN is a startup founder and investor born in Brooklyn and raised in suburban Maryland. After graduating from the University of Virginia in 2005, Alexis and his co-founder, Steve Huffman, started reddit, one of the hundred most popular websites in the world. Now a reddit board member, Alexis focuses on the social enterprise Breadpig, which publishes the world's most popular webcomics, such as *xkcd*, *Dinosaur Comics*, and *Saturday Morning Breakfast Cereal*. All Breadpig's profits are donated to worthy causes. Alexis helped launch the travel website hipmunk and ran its marketing, PR, and community operations before becoming an adviser and joining the fight against the Stop Online Piracy Act and the PROTECT IP Act.

Alexis invests in and advises more than sixty tech startups and continues to advocate for Internet freedom. He's Y Combinator's ambassador to the East and co-founder of the nonprofit Institute on Higher Awesome Studies. Along the way, Alexis has spoken at the TED Conference and at other conferences and universities worldwide. He spent three months volunteering in Armenia as a Kiva Fellow and was named twice to the *Forbes* 30 under 30 list. He lives on the Internet, but his tax documents still go to Brooklyn.

Alexis wants to know what you thought of his book and how you'll use it to be awesome! Let him know via Twitter @alexisohanian.

**BUSINESS
PLUS**

Recognized as one of the world's most prestigious business imprints, Business Plus specializes in publishing books that are on the cutting edge. Like you, to be successful we always strive to be ahead of the curve.

Business Plus titles encompass a wide range of books and interests—including important business management works, state-of-the-art personal financial advice, noteworthy narrative accounts, the latest in sales and marketing advice, individualized career guidance, and autobiographies of the key business leaders of our time.

Our philosophy is that business is truly global in every way, and that today's business reader is looking for books that are both entertaining and educational. To find out more about what we're publishing, please check out the Business Plus blog at:

www.businessplusbooks.com